Literature Instruction

PRACTICE

AND

POLICY

Literature Instruction

PRACTICE

AND

POLICY

EDITED BY

James Flood

Judith A. Langer

SCHOLASTIC

LEADERSHIP
POLICY
RESEARCH ™

New York • Toronto • London • Auckland • Sydney

ISBN 0–590–49756–1

12 11 10 9 8 7 6 5 4 3 2 1   1 2 3 4 5 / 9

Printed in the U.S.A.

Library of Congress Cataloging-in-Publication Data

Literature instruction: practice and policy/edited by James Flood
    and Judith A. Langer.
        p.   cm.
    Includes bibliographical references.
    ISBN 0–590–49756–1
    1. Literature—Study and teaching (Elementary)—United States.
2. Literature—Study and teaching (Secondary)—United States.
    I. Flood, James. II. Langer, Judith A.
LB1575.5U5L59   1994
372.64'0973—dc20   93-39342
                                                        CIP

Designed by Joan Gazdik Gillner

PREFACE

THIS VOLUME WAS DEVELOPED AS AN EXPLORATION of recent findings from research concerned with the teaching of literature in contemporary classrooms. The papers contained in this volume speak to the issues involved in the successful teaching of literature.

Each author addresses a complex issue in the teaching and learning of literature. With the first two papers, one written by Judith Langer and and the other by Sheridan Blau, the stage is set for the volume with an examination of current views about reader-based instruction—that is, examining the role of the reader rather than the text as the primary focus of instruction. Each author investigates the ways in which theory moves into practice in real classrooms. These two pieces are followed by a paper by Purcell-Gates in which she looks at the ways that young children become members of the literary community.

The remainder of the papers discuss some of the most controversial and critical issues in literature instruction today. Nancy Roser raises and answers key questions in the debate about beginning literacy instruction—appreciation of great literary texts versus the acquisition and practice of basic skills. Violet Harris discusses the issues involved in the inclusion of multicultural literature in the curriculum, and Jim Marshall talks about the deleterious effects of ability grouping in literature instruction.

Alan Purves discusses the unexamined and unresolved issues involved in assessing literature teaching and learning, and Jim Squire raises questions of public policy and literature teaching. Squire challenges the literature establishment to discuss the role of government in literature education. In the final paper, Flood and Lapp discuss the ingredients necessary for establishing widespread change in contemporary literature instruction.

The volume is intended for teachers of literature as well as students of the teaching of literature. Critical questions are raised, emerging insights and recommendations are offered, and new questions are posed. We hope you enjoy as much as we have the exploration of these complex and challenging questions .

James Flood
Judith Langer

TABLE OF CONTENTS

CHAPTER 1

CHAPTER

READER-BASED
LITERATURE INSTRUCTION

Judith A. Langer

University at Albany, State University of New York

AFTER SOME THIRTY YEARS OF RELATIVE neglect we are beginning to witness a needed resurgence of attention to theory and practice in literature instruction. The last wave of change in elementary and secondary school teaching of literature took place in the early 1960s in response to New Critical theory (e.g., Brooks, 1947; Welleck & Warren, 1949), which taught students to do close reading of texts with particular emphasis on the narrator, the point of view, and the "correct" interpretation. Such an approach is text based, considering the locus of understanding to reside within the work and the students' abilities to arrive at understanding to reside in their manipulations of the text for the meaning it brings. This is dramatically different from a process view of reading, writing, and instruction, which treats the student as an active meaning-seeker, continually transacting with the text in order to create an interpretation (Iser, 1978; Rosenblatt 1938, 1978).

This latter view regards the text as a mere blueprint (rather than an exacting recipe), marking paths of possible meaning that can be actualized only in the mind of the reader. Thus the potential for more than one "correct" interpretation is created. In this view, instruction focuses on the defensibility of meanings students arrive at and on the ways in which they build, refine, elaborate, and communicate that meaning rather than on a particular desired response. Although reader-based theory has received a good deal of pedagogical attention in recent years and teachers say they want their students to think as well as analyze and remember (Marshall, 1989, 1990), a New Critical approach toward instruction still dominates American literature instruction (Applebee, 1992, in press; Applebee & Purves, 1992). As a result, the English classroom is in conceptual disarray, using a student-centered process approach to writing instruction on the one hand and a text-centered product approach to literature instruction on the other. This has happened despite the many national as well as local calls for an academic focus on developing students' thinking and reasoning abilities. While reader response theory is compatible with student-centered process approaches and has therefore been embraced as an alternative approach to instruction (see Langer, 1989, 1990a, 1990b, 1990c; Probst, 1988; Dias, 1990; Dias & Hayhoe, 1988; California Literature Framework, 1987), it remains a university-based critical theory—not yet sufficiently rethought as a pedagogical theory to lead to widespread reform of instructional practices in English/language arts classes.

Since 1987, with the establishment of the Center for the Learning and Teaching of Literature, my work has focused on the processes involved in understanding literature and on ways we can more productively help students become rich thinkers about and responders to literature. My goal has been to develop an alternative pedagogy, one that can replace the existing text-centered one. This is needed because the practices that presently underlie literature instruction—curriculum goals, assessment practices, and most instructional materials—still value students' recall of facts and their learning of received interpretations more than their ability to engage in *literary experiences*—responding to, exploring, and enriching their own interpretations. Thus, even in this era of educational reform that ostensibly supports students' reasoning abilities and despite the dramatic changes that have taken place in the teaching of writing, rethinking literature instruction from a "process of thinking" approach is, to a large degree, just beginning.

For the past few years, through my work at the Literature Center, I have been developing a reader-based theory for the teaching of literature—one that can help us understand what it means to make sense of literature from a reader's point of view and what that means for refocusing our instructional goals and practices. One part of my work (Langer, 1989, 1990a) helps explain the process of literary understanding. It suggests that when readers engage in a literary experience, their cognitive orientations can be characterized as *reaching toward a horizon of possibilities.* As soon as they begin to read or discuss a piece, they have a sense of the whole piece (what it will be about and how it might end), but that sense of the whole is fluid, always changing. As they make sense of new ideas, readers immediately turn them on end, creating uncertainty by exploring what those ideas might mean in terms of the characters' interactions, feelings, intentions, or actions, or in terms of particular events—as the readers understand them at that moment. In addition, readers take these explorations and consider how they might affect the way the piece might end. It is the raising of questions and the exploration of possibilities that lie at the heart of a literary reading, and it is a mixture of understandings and uncertainties that readers come away with at the end of a piece. Yet, too often instruction treats the reading of literature as information getting, expecting completed knowledge—after students have read the last line—to be recited and evaluated (for "accuracy") in class.

I will discuss some of what I have been learning from a six-year study carried out in collaboration with forty middle and high school teachers from both urban and suburban communities. We have been trying to understand the pedagogical principles that underlie instruction when classrooms become environments that encourage students to arrive at their own understandings, explore possibilities, and move beyond their initial understandings to more thoughtful interpretations. (See Langer, 1990b, 1990c, 1992a, 1992b for a detailed explanation of the studies and findings.)

During the project, each teacher found her or his own way to encourage students to engage in the process of literary understanding at least some of the time. Further, when this occurred, the classrooms became cultural contexts that both called for and expected the active thought and participation of each student. These classrooms had a number of characteristics that I will discuss briefly: (1) each treated the reading of literature as a process of "coming to understand"—with the students' initial ideas as a place to begin to think more deeply about the piece; (2) each treated class meetings as a time to discuss and for ideas to grow; thus, students' concerns were at the heart of the discussion, and writing as well as discussion was used as a way to stimulate and support students' growing understandings; and (3) each treated literary understanding as the exploration of possibilities; therefore, evaluation of factual knowledge was inappropriate to the goals of the lessons while seeking and weighing evidence and learning to explain, defend, elaborate, and refine understandings and to compare them to others' interpretations were at the heart of the instruction.

• Reading as a Process of Coming to Understand •

In situations where the students were thoughtfully engaged in developing and enriching their own responses, their teachers focused on the "envisionments" the students were building. Envisionments are the changing text worlds students form in their minds as they read, discuss, think, and write about a piece. Instruction was driven by the underlying belief that readers' understandings change and grow with time, even after the reading has ended, and that students need to learn to become aware of their own changing and growing envisionments. Because the teachers were guided by the assumption that all students are in the process of making sense of what they read and that they need to learn to reflect on and reconsider these meanings, the students were treated as thinkers, as if they could and would have interesting, cogent thoughts about the pieces they read as well as questions they would like to discuss. In supporting the process of building on what the students were envisioning, the teachers provided the students with ownership for the topics of discussion, making the students' understandings the central focus of each class meeting.

Sharing Initial Impressions. This focus on student understandings was the teachers' primary concern, right from the opening of the class discussion, when the students' initial impressions were sought and continuing through the project. In the following excerpt from a suburban high school class discussion, we can see how Sharon Burns, the teacher, makes it clear from the activities she assigns and questions she asks early in the year that it is the students' understandings she is after. After her students had read a portion of *Catcher in the Rye*, they met in groups to discuss their initial thoughts and questions. These became the focus of the whole class discussion:

TEACHER: I heard lots of good things as I was going around.
. . . Who wants to begin? . . .

JOE: We all agreed that Holden is unpredictable.

TEACHER: Okay. Why?

JOE: Why? Because what she said (pointing to another student), she said that he, like, does one thing and he'll just turn around and do the total opposite.

TEACHER: Like what?

SCOTT: Like, he's really honest with himself about things and he, like, knows what he expects of himself and what he believes. Might be a liar to someone else. Like, he'll lie to other people.

JEN: He lies.

TEACHER: Kind of contradicts himself, but does this bother you about his lying?

JEN/SCOTT: No.

TEACHER: Tell me about it.

In this case and others like it, such experiences prompted class discussions that began with the students' envisionments, permitting them to voice their initial responses, to hear those of others, and to extend and develop their overall understanding. While the teacher's questions are not new (teachers have always asked students to explain themselves), it is the intent underlying the questions—the answers the teacher is after—that make the difference. For example, someone unfamiliar with Sharon's instructional views could interpret her question "Okay, why?" as either a call for the students to guess what response the teacher was after or as a prompt for the students' own thoughtful responses. The intent would depend on whether the teacher wants and accepts the students' own developing interpretations or a predetermined "right" answer. In this case, Sharon uses the students' initial impressions as the way to focus her lessons, using their ideas to extend the dialogue and prompt the students to think further. It is the students' ideas she is after and their incomplete (and growing) understandings she considers as appropriate responses to her questions. This is conveyed over time, by her continued invitations to students to contribute their ideas (e.g., "Like what? Tell me about it.") and by her lack of telling.

Similarly Barbara Furst, a middle school teacher in a suburban community, began her class discussion of *All Summer in a Day* by Ray Bradbury with the following question:

> I want to ask you to remember back when you finished reading the story yesterday, when you got to the end of the story, what were you thinking about? What were you feeling as you got to the end of the story? Do you remember? Patricia?

Because Patricia knew her teacher was not after a plot summary or a theme statement but a statement of her own personal response at the end of the reading, she responded accordingly.

> PATRICIA: I thought that she was still kind of irresponsible (mumble) for such a long time. And, I think I was wondering if she found out about Margo and if she did anything.
>
> TEACHER: Okay, so you were trying to imagine what was going to happen. . . . Michelle?

Thus the class meeting centered on the students' concerns; throughout the entire lesson, Barbara used the students' comments to help them discuss their own initial impressions. She ended the lesson by preparing the students to see a film of the story the next day, letting them know their understandings remained the focus, and would be discussed at the next possible meeting:

> [A]s you watch the film, do the same thing you were doing when you were reading the story. . . . [write] what you're thinking. So, if something happens on the screen, what are you thinking about what happens? You know, is this different, why did it change? Have you got a question, "I didn't see it this way"? On Monday we can talk about those two questions.

• Class Meetings as Time to Work Through Understandings •

Because the students' concerns were at the heart of the class discussions, the teachers helped them think through their ideas (as Sharon was beginning to do when she asked her class if they were bothered by Holden's lying), supporting them toward richer interpretations. To do this, the teachers asked questions that prompted the students to probe what they were envisioning, rather than focusing on teacher or text-generated content that was external to the students' concerns.

Using student knowledge taps to support thoughtful discussion. The kinds of questions we came to call "student knowledge taps" were questions designed to tap what the students understood and to prompt them to consider these more fully. They were questions that had no single right answers, and they also prompted extended language and thought about the issues troubling the students. However, this does not mean that there was no check on the students' understandings, nor that "anything goes." In fact, the teachers elicited the students' envisionments, and then guided them to question and clarify their ideas. This is very different from telling. The following example from the same discussion of *Catcher in the Rye* in Sharon's class illustrates the kinds of questions the teachers asked to help the students rethink their ideas, maintaining students' building of their understandings as the focus of the lesson:

JAMIE: To him it's not a major thing in the world about whether you're lying or not. Like his sister and brother died and stuff. And so, like he, so he goes, what the heck. . . .

TEACHER: Okay, Matt?

MATT: I think he's just trying to hide from his past and what happened.

FERN: Their freedom?

TEACHER: Okay. So tell me more.

CAROL: He might not want to talk about either.

MATT: I don't know. Either that or he just does it to amuse himself.

TEACHER: Okay, either to hide something or to amuse himself. Did he used to wear a hat?

MATT: Yeah. Sure. He always had that hat.

TEACHER: What did he do with it? He loved that hat. He wore it backwards.

MATT: He gave it to his sister. To get attention. To change character.

TEACHER: What do you mean? . . .

JAMIE: . . . It says he likes being normal and kind of joking around, goofing around, being immature. Didn't it say that?

TEACHER: Okay. So that's just his personality. Is he a bad person?

Sharon uses such questions throughout this part of the discussion to help the students think more deeply about whether Holden was a liar because he was an essentially bad person or whether he had psychological demons he had to contend with, a question they had raised.

Neither Sharon nor the other teachers who used such questioning strategies had one particular interpretation in mind; they did not ask "leading" questions that inched the students toward one sanctioned response. Instead, they used student knowledge taps as ways to stimulate the students' own thinking about topics they themselves had already brought up.

In fact, one teacher explained that whenever she rereads a piece and has her class discuss it she gets something somewhat different from each experience and she wants her students to be able to do the same.

Using Writing to Support Understanding. Besides discussion, a variety of writing activities, taking forms as diverse as logs, briefwrites, informal letters, reviews, written conversations, essays, and analytic papers supported students' envisionment-building. Such experiences encouraged them to reflect on, state, defend, and rethink their envisionments and to form their own interpretations. For example, the students were often asked to keep literature journals. In one seventh grade urban class, the students were encouraged to write thought-provoking questions to discuss in class. (Teacher: "Write thoughtful questions, not things we could just look up." and also "Make a prediction in your journal when you put the book down. Check it later to see if that happened.") Response journals were also used as preparation for whole class discussion (Teacher, seventh grade urban: "I'm going to give you five minutes. Look through your journal. Use it as a jumping off place to get an overview of your ideas. Jot down a question you want to ask.").

Cyrus Ford, an eleventh grade city teacher, asked his students to write what "Marty," the play they had read, meant to them. Selected papers (anonymous) were read to the class and served as the impetus for discussion. While in other kinds of writing the students tended to build upon and ponder their understandings, in this type of writing they often used their envisionments to reflect on their own lives and experiences.

For example, Thomas wrote:

To me, the play says that you shouldn't let anyone decide who your friends are going to be, except you. I have learned from the characters that if you feel good about something and believe in it, then you should go for it, and not let anyone or anything stand in the way. . . .

Moneisha wrote:

To me the play expresses the fact that no matter what people think, you have to follow your heart, and Marty is trying to make his life complete. Mother is beginning to worry about when Marty gets married, what is to become of her. My opinion of the play has changed somewhat since the beginning of the play. At first I thought Marty would die an old lonely fat man. But it seems Marty is going to get married. . . .

Writing was also used as a way to help the students record the ideas and questions they had when they were reading alone, so they could reflect on them at a later time, perhaps in class discussion. For example, when reading and discussing *All Summer in a Day*, Barbara Furst said to her class:

If you notice something that you're reading, something about the language, something about the way the characters behave, something about the way the story is written, something you don't understand, something that is confusing to you, anything that you have a comment about as well as any questions you have, I'd like you to put that on your paper. . . . In our discussion group, I want to be able to talk about the story, but I also want to talk about what you were thinking, what kinds of thinking you were doing as you read the story.

• Literary Understanding as the Exploration of Possibilities •

Because the teachers' viewed building on what the students envisioned in literary contexts as involving the exploration of possibilities, instruction focused on helping students become inquisitive and discern possibilities from their own understandings as well as from their knowledge of the human situation. The teachers assumed that after completing a piece, students come away with questions as well as understandings, and that responding to litera-ture *involves* the raising of questions. Instruction, therefore, helped students not merely to resolve their own uncertainties, but to go beyond—considering alternatives and weighing the evidence.

Barbara, the middle school teacher mentioned above, spent an entire session helping her students gain richer understandings of *All Summer in a Day* by exploring possibilities—in this case by first thinking about Margo. Here, Barbara encourages the students to explore possible interpretations and then check their plausibility by referring to the text:

ROBIN: Well, I was thinking that, like, they open up the closet and Margo wasn't there, and she got out somehow. And, like, they never, I wanted that to happen, that Margo got out and they never heard from her again, and she saw reality in the sun (mumble). That's what I wanted to happen.

TEACHER: All right, based on the story, what do you think happened?

ROBIN: I think she would probably just come out and not say a word, and just start crying, because even though she missed the sun, just then she still has seen the sun more than they have.

TEACHER: All right, what makes you think she'd react that way? What do you know about Margo?

JIM: Because she isn't, like, a person with a bad tem-per that would come up and just start beating everybody up and stuff. 'Cause she's just, like, quiet and a little shy, and you don't picture her like that.

TEACHER: . . . He's saying, based on what he knows about Margo's character, he thinks she would come out of the closet crying or not saying anything.

JIM: Just like, they would be saying sorry or every-thing and she would just, like, be silent, because she doesn't have much to say. She's just, like, a quiet person, and I don't think I could picture her, like, screaming and yelling.

TEACHER: All right. Pete?

PETE: I kind of think that Margaret is a little crazy and isn't playing with a full deck, and that this is the kind of thing that would push her over the edge. . . .

TEACHER: Pete, you think that she's very close to the edge. What in the story makes you think that?

PETE: The part where she wants the sun so bad, and that she refused to take a shower because she didn't want the water to touch her head, and that she wasn't thinking clearly. A little weird.

They go on to explore possible interpretations of other parts of the story as well. Later, for instance:

PATRICIA: They let her out and realized she was right.

TEACHER: So you're saying that the children are going to be a little different at the end because they're going to realize that Margo was right. Now we're looking at something else here. . . . Robin?

ROBIN: I think that she knew that the sun already came out because before she went into the closet it was barely raining out, and when she came out it was, like, coming out really hard.

TEACHER: Jeff, you bring up the issue of the children feeling guilty. Is there anything in the story, is there any clue that the author gives you that there might be some guilt on the part of the children?

ERIC: In the last paragraph . . .

ROBERT: 'Cause they're all going, "Go, go ahead. What are you waiting for?" And you can tell the kids are like (mumble).

Similarly, almost all of the teachers continually reinforced the notion that the reading of literature involves the generation of questions by encouraging their students to come to class prepared to ask their questions. An eleventh grade urban teacher explained this directly to the class:

When you read literature there are many unanswered questions. In time and sometimes through talking some of these become clearer. But there are always questions. It's part of the way your mind works when you read literature. It's part of what makes it interesting—even exciting.

Minds on task. Because so large a portion of the literature lessons involved interactions of all sorts (before, during, and after reading; in pairs, small groups, and whole class; with and without the teacher), the issue of the "silent" students, those who are quiet by nature as well as those for whom the reading assignment poses difficulty, becomes an important consideration. It soon became clear, however, that in these instructional environments, the kinds of thinking the students did rather than the amount they talked was of ultimate value. Analyses of videotapes and fieldnotes of lessons indicate that while the quiet students were invited to join the conversations, their need to be left alone was respected; they were given the room to enter the conversation when they were ready. For them, quiet time was not lost time, but minds on time. During these periods, they spent a good deal of time listening to and responding to the ideas they heard; they were rapt in thought even though they did not speak aloud. It was as if they were engaged in silent participation, where they used the ideas expressed by others to advance their own private negotiations of meaning. Sometimes these students spoke aloud but often not until the late in the discussions. And when they spoke, they had something to say. They agreed and disagreed with what others had said, raised new possibilities, and sometimes even upped the ante by raising complexities not yet addressed. It became apparent that their silent times had not been off task, but rather opportunities for them to ponder others' understandings that initially were more complete, more fluent, or simply different from their own (although sometimes the same); to see the processes of literary thinking as well as literary discussion (see Langer, 1992b) modeled for them; and to publicly try out such ideas and strategies when they felt comfortable doing so, in a supportive as well as instructive (see Langer, 1990c) environment.

• Toward Meaningful Reform •

In the classrooms I have described, students were given room to work through their ideas in a variety of contexts: in whole class discussion, alone, and in groups—in reading, writing, and speaking. Developing envisionments, exploring them, talking about them, and refining understandings underlay the very fabric of the social interactions that defined being a class member. Although other people's interpretations were discussed and considered, they were introduced and analyzed only after the students had had an opportunity to explore their own interpretations. Thus, they were able to react to other ideas (including received interpretations) through the lens of their own considered understandings—which continued to be treated conditionally, always subject to further development.

In instructional contexts of this sort, ones that treat all students as thinkers and provide them with the environment as well as the help to do this, even the most "at risk" students can engage in thoughtful discussions about literature, develop rich and deep understandings—and enjoy it, too. But other Literature Center projects indicate that literature instruction tends not to be like the kind I've described. Arthur Applebee's (1989) national surveys of literature instruction, for instance, indicate that literature lessons generally stress facts and "correct" interpretations, and when students' responses are sought, they are generally used at the beginning of lessons, for motivation. Then they get on with the "real," text-based lesson.

Alan Purves' (Brody, DeMilo, & Purves, 1989) studies of literature tests, both formal and informal, show that most test questions treat knowing literature as getting the right answer. (His favorite standardized test question is: Huck Finn is a good boy. True or False.) Neither in teaching nor testing do students have much opportunity to share what they understand or to explore possibilities.

Clearly, change is needed. The chapters that follow are part of the growing dialogue that will inform our decisions. Instead of being merely reactive, each focuses on a particular concern, explaining theoretical dimensions underlying the pragmatic solutions that are posed. Together, they offer a mosaic of suggestions for change, all from a student-centered view of literary reading and understanding. In this first chapter, I have suggested three broad principles of instruction that characterize the pedagogical theory underlying reader-based instruction. They can be used to conceptualize notions of learning and teaching suggested by each of the chapters to follow.

REFERENCES

Applebee, A. (1992). The background for reform. In J. Langer (Ed.), *Literature instruction: A focus on student response.* Urbana, IL: National Council of Teachers of English.

Applebee, A.N. (in press). *Literature in the secondary school.* Urbana, IL: National Council of Teachers of English.

Applebee, A.N., and Purves, A. (1992). Curriculum research in literature and the other language arts. In P. Jackson (Ed.), *Handbook of research on curriculum.* New York: Macmillan.

Bradbury, R. (1959). All summer in a day. In *A medicine for melancholy.* Garden City, NY: Doubleday.

Brody, P., DeMilo, C., & Purves, A. (1989). *The current state of assessment in literature* (Report Series 3.1). Albany, NY: Center for the Learning and Teaching of Literature.

Brooks, C. (1947). *The well wrought urn: Studies in the structure of poetry.* New York: Harcourt, Brace & Co.

California Department of Education. (1987). *English-language arts framework for California public schools, kindergarten through grade 12.* Sacramento: California State Department of Education.

Chayefsky, P. (1983). Marty. In O.S. Niles, E.J. Farrell, & R.M. LeBlanc (Eds.), *Album, USA* (pp. 92–119). Glenview, IL: Scott Foresman & Co. (Original work published in 1955).

Dias, P. (1990). *Literary reading and classroom constraints: Aligning practice with theory* (Report Series 5.2). Albany, NY: Center for Learning and Teaching of Literature.

Dias, P., & Hayhoe, M. (1988). *Developing response to poetry.* Philadelphia: Open University Press.

Langer, J.A. (1989). *The process of understanding literature* (Report Series 2.1). Albany, NY: Center for the Learning and Teaching of Literature.

Langer. J.A. (1990a). The process of understanding: Reading for literary and informative purposes. *Research in the Teaching of English, 24* (3), 229–260.

Langer, J.A. (1990b). Understanding literature. *Language Arts, 812–816.*

Langer, J.A. (1990c). *Literary understanding and literature instruction* (Report Series 2.11). Albany, NY: Center for the Learning and Teaching of Literature.

Langer, J.A. (1992a). Rethinking literature instruction. In J. Langer (Ed.), *Literature instruction: A focus on student response.* Urbana, IL: National Council of Teachers of English.

Langer, J.A. (1992b). Discussion as exploration: Literature and the horizon of possibilities. In G. Newell and R. Durst (Eds.), *Exploring texts: The role of discussion and writing in the teaching of literature.* Norwood, MA: Christopher Gordon Publishers.

Iser, W. (1978). *The act of reading.* Baltimore: The Johns Hopkins Press.

Marshall, J. (1989). *Patterns of discourse in classroom discussions of literature* (Report Series 2.9). Albany, NY: Center for the Learning and Teaching of Literature.

Marshall, J. (1990). *Discussions of literature in lower-track classrooms* (Report Series 2.10). Albany, NY: Center for the Learning and Teaching of Literature.

Probst, R. (1988). *Response and analysis: Teaching literature in junior and senior high school.* Portsmouth, NH: Boynton/Cook.

Rosenblatt, L. (1938). *Literature as exploration* (4th ed.). New York: Modern Language Association.

Rosenblatt, L. (1978). *The reader, the text, and the poem.* Cambridge: Harvard University Press.

Salinger, D.H. (1951). *Catcher in the rye.* Boston: Little, Brown & Company.

Welleck, R., & Warren, A. (1949). *Theory of literature.* New York: Harcourt Brace.

CHAPTER 2

TRANSACTIONS BETWEEN THEORY AND PRACTICE IN THE TEACHING OF LITERATURE

Sheridan Blau
University of California at Santa Barbara

T HIS CHAPTER EXPLORES A PARTICULAR professional development model for teachers of literature (K–13) in the context of current disjunctions between literary theory and pedagogical practices in the teaching of literature on the one hand, and a different set of disjunctions between teaching practices in literature and in composition on the other. At the center of the discussion is the story of what happened when a community of experienced English and language arts teachers, representing all grades from elementary school through college, collaborated through an NEH-sponsored Literature Institute for Teachers to study (with guidance from leading specialists in literature and in pedagogy) a number of difficult literary texts. In addition to studying the literature, they examined their own processes as readers of literature, reflected on their own teaching methods, and learned about recent developments in literary theory and critical practice.

The point of the story is that teachers of literature who are experiencing what Judith Langer (1990) has described as a "schizophrenic" split between process-oriented approaches to teaching writing on the one hand and right-answer approaches to teaching literature on the other can and will liberate themselves from conventional teaching practices in literature. The teacher will abandon conventional practices (which are also inconsistent with recent perspectives in literary theory) when they have the opportunity to experiment with alternative reading and teaching practices and to construct a coherent theoretical framework that sanctions and supports their expanding pedagogical repertoire.

The story of this particular NEH project is significant because it presents a model for the professional development of teachers of literature at a particularly problematic moment in English education—a moment when the sophistication of our profession in the teaching of literature is not only two decades out of touch with literary theory and criticism but a decade behind our sophistication in the teaching of writing. This problem occurs when many of the teachers who are most expert in the teaching of writing find their goals and methods for teaching literature inconsistent with the process-oriented pedagogy they have come to implement in their teaching of composition. Whatever professional progress may have taken place during the past decade in the teaching of writing, the teaching of literature appears to remain largely text-centered rather than student-centered, competitive rather than collaborative, and product-oriented rather than process-oriented (see James Marshall's 1989 study of secondary school literature teachers, and Don Zancanella's related 1991 study of junior high teachers). Why such conditions should exist, why we might want to change them, how we can go about making the appropriate changes, and what a more satisfying set of literary teaching practices would look like are the principal subjects of this chapter.

THE CRITICAL CLIMATE FOR THE CURRENT PREDICAMENT

• New Criticism •

Let me begin my account of the present predicament in the teaching of literature by providing a rough and rapid sketch—"on one foot," as ancient exegetes would say—of the main currents of literary theory and criticism over the past forty or so years. This will help us see how recent developments in literary theory and criticism have challenged and puzzled almost two generations of teachers who were educated according to a set of critical practices that were revolutionary and unsettling to the academic community of the 1940s and '50s but that now represent "old-fashioned," if not discredited, practice. For most active literature teachers over the age of forty, this will be the story of our lives as students, readers, and teachers (also see Lynn, 1990).

The now old-fashioned but once newfangled literary culture out of which—or against which—critical theories and practices of the past twenty or twenty-five years have emerged is the culture dominated by what we still know as the "New Criticism." The New Criticism was "new" because in the decades of the '40s and '50s, when it was championed by its most influential exponents (W.K. Wimsatt, Cleanth Brooks, Randall Jarrell, and John Crowe Ransom, among others), it represented a set of critical practices that were proposed to replace an earlier critical tradition that had emphasized the biography of the writer, the historical or theological contexts for particular works, the moral and ethical enlightenment conferred upon readers, and the highly impressionistic and "appreciative" accounts of the aesthetic and ethical features of literary works (see Wellek &

Warren, 1956 [1949], p.127). The New Criticism was a formalist criticism because it emphasized the formal features of a literary text. It treated the text as an artifact, something constructed and subject first to objective, scientific description and then to an evaluation based on observable features (see Brooks, 1947, especially Appendix I). It is no accident, I think, that formalist literary criticism emerged most forcefully in the 1950s simultaneously with formalist or descriptive linguistics, which sought to provide scientifically accurate accounts of the workings of specific languages.

New Critics were inclined to forgo discussions of an author's biography and the background for literary works in favor of a discourse that honored the "integrity" of a literary text, its coherence as a unified artifact whose every detail must be regarded as meaningful, whether consciously intended by the artist or not. For John Ciardi (1959), who attempted to build a program for teaching poetry based on New Critical principles, a poem was a performance of itself in time and space, a formal structure, which he delighted in defining as "one thing against another across a silence." The job of the reader or critic of such an artifact was to apprehend all of its features (to engage in "close reading") and to uncover the structures of meaning that informed the text, particularly revealing the ironies and paradoxes that create "tensions" and explicating the "unity" that resolved those tensions. In this enterprise, which was typically as much an evaluative as an interpretive one, critics were expected to conduct inquiries in a way that was finely tuned to the emotional nuances of their own reading experiences, yet to do so in a spirit akin to scientific objectivity, eschewing any response to the text that might represent the biases or special pleading of any particular reader or group of readers.

To attend to a text as a New Critic, then, was to treat the text, in

Wimsatt's memorable title phrase, as a *Verbal Icon* (1954), an object requiring an almost religious devotion, if one wanted to apprehend all its features and account for how those features produced a particular set of meanings—meanings that might be said to inhere distinctively and uniquely in this particular self-contained structure—that is, the text. Students and critics of such icons would dutifully devote themselves to producing detailed, objective studies of image patterns, word frequencies, and so on in the interest of showing how every detail of a text conspired to produce a unified work of art with a determinable, if not final, meaning (cf. Wellek & Warren's description of a literary work as a stratified system of norms that the reader attempts to grasp, p.139).

Yet, since meaning was conceived of as an integral function of a unique formal structure—the concrete particulars that constituted a literary work—it would be fallacious to attempt to abstract a meaning from a text as if it were detachable from the formal operations through which it was realized. Thus, John Ciardi used to insist, "we talk about the meaning of a poem only when we don't know what else to say abut it." For Ciardi, as for the school of New Critics whose principles he made available to a generation of high school and college students, the essential question for readers or interpreters of literary works was not "what does a poem mean?" but the question that he used as the title of his widely taught textbook, *How Does a Poem Mean* (1959).

As much as the New Criticism may be said to represent a set of prescribed reading practices, it may be even more characteristically associated with a set of critical proscriptions—that is, with an opposition to a number of alternative critical practices that it was a reaction to or in competition with. These were characteristically classified by practitioners of New Criticism, following the example of Wimsatt and Beardsley (1954), as critical "fallacies" or even "heresies," including the most famous pair: "the intentional fallacy," locating textual meaning in the determinable intentions of an author, and "the affective fallacy," locating meaning in the way a text affects readers. Other spokesmen (they were virtually all men) for the New Criticism warned teachers and students alike against the temptations of what became commonly referred to as "the biographical heresy" (interpreting a poem, for example, as an autobiographical document), "the political heresy" (allowing political values or class biases to influence interpretations or judgments of literary value), "the moralist herasy" (allowing ethical or moral judgments to substitute for aesthetic criteria in determining literary value), "the psychological fallacy" (interpreting a literary work as an expression of an author's unconscious drives and preoccupations), and what Cleanth Brooks (1947) called "the heresy of paraphrase" (the idea that works ought to be valued or even discussed largely in terms of their paraphraseable content).

Virtually all of these critical heresies or fallacies were represented by the practice of some critics and scholars of the period (including such leading literary figures as Yvor Winters, C.S. Lewis, and Leslie Fiedler), and it is surely the case that the most eminent practicing critics and literary scholars who associated themselves and their pedagogy with the New Criticism would not have hesitated to avail themselves of any perspective on a literary work that promised to illuminate a text they were interested in. Nonetheless, teachers raised on the New Criticism (whether they were aware of their critical heritage or not) were inclined to avoid certain practices in their teaching or to feel apologetic for practices that could be associated with one of the critical heresies. In my own teaching career, for example, I used to feel apologetic and was sometimes criticized by observers for "getting away from the text" in my lectures and class discussions. It was not that I spent class time discussing extraneous topics but that I often asked students to consider how they had personally experienced psychological states or moral dilemmas in their own lives analogous to those described in the literary works we were studying. Class discussions therefore entailed stories told by students about personal experiences associated with the fictive events we were reading. And such discussions were seen as violating a pedagogical principle derived from a narrow conception of New Critical doctrine: that the text itself—the words that appear on the page rather than such related discourses as parallel stories by students—must remain the exclusive focus of discourse in instruction.

• Postmodern or Poststructuralist Criticism •

By the late sixties and more vigorously in the following two decades there emerged on the critical scene a variety of highly influential literary theories that self-consciously defined themselves as oppositional to New Critical doctrine and that almost perversely embodied the various fallacies and heresies conventionally proscribed by the New Critics. It was almost as if each of the fallacies or heresies that New Criticism had discarded now sprouted like the teeth of a dragon into an autonomous literary theory seeking to supplant the New Criticism in eminence and authority.

Two of the earliest and most explicit American challengers to the hegemony of the New Criticism were E.D. Hirsch and Stanley Fish, whose major critical works in 1967 and 1968, respectively, turned the intentional fallacy and the affective fallacy into authoritative standards for literary interpretation. Hirsch's *Validity in Interpretation* (1967) argued that authorial intention is not only relevant to the interpretive enterprise but constitutes the only valid source of authority for an interpretation. Without such authority, he insisted, the entire field of literary criticism is reduced to a game of rhetoric without standards for evaluating the validity of one claim over another. In the following year Fish published *Surprised By Sin:*

The Reader in Paradise Lost, an account of how the meaning of Milton's epic can be found in the intellectual and emotional temptations to which an attentive reader succumbs psychologically in the course of reading the poem. In his introduction to the book, Fish acknowledges that his critical method may be attacked as an enactment of the affective fallacy, but that, if he is guilty of such treason, he is willing to make the most of it!

With Fish's rebellious gesture against his literary mentors, American reader-response theory was inaugurated as a respectable, though still controversial, school of criticism that quickly moved toward an increased emphasis on the role of the reader as a kind of cowriter of the text being read—at the least an active participant in the construction of whatever meaning may be attributed to a text. For many practicing critics who now align themselves with reader-response theory, a work of literature is an inert text that can hardly be said to have more than a potential for meaning until it is called into being by a reader who constructs a reading, thereby giving meaning to the text. A single text (like a musical score) may therefore be performed or construed in as many ways as there are readers (or communities of readers) to perform it.

Such an endorsement of the subjectivity and relativism that New Criticism sought to protect against was only the first wave of the attack that theorists of the past two decades have launched as part of the larger postmodern or poststructuralist project to disestablish the authority of the text. In doing so, they have moved to desanctify the verbal icon in favor of the more pluralistic and problematic authority of readers, particularly situated readers—which is to say biased readers, who read from the particular perspectives they occupy by virtue of their race, class, gender, ideology, personal experience, psychological profile, academic training, and historical location. Thus, aside from the school of reader-response theorists (see

Tompkins, 1980), which would include such critics as the continental theorist Wolfgang Iser (1978), the rediscovered Louise Rosenblatt (whose pioneering work in 1938, *Literature as Exploration*, was generally ignored outside the field of teacher education prior to the emergence in University English departments of an important school of reader-response theorists), Fish himself, and the subjectivist critic David Bleich (1978), there developed in the decades of the 1970s and 1980s a variety of critical schools identified by their particular situated identities—all of them methodologically committed to one or another of the fallacies or heresies anathematized by New Critics. These would include such critical schools as those of the Marxists, the feminists, and others that might identify themselves with "cultural criticism" broadly conceived. Such critics have presented cogent arguments for the re-evaluation of the literary canon from feminist or non-Eurocentric perspectives and have urged readers to recognize the ways in which literary texts implicate their readers in racially biased, class-biased, or gender-biased cultural assumptions.

Feminists have pointed out, for example (Schweickart, 1986), that many of the poems most favored and most taught (by a predominantly male faculty in literature) to undergraduate literature students (most of whom are women) are poems that express admiration for the bodies of women, poems which, quite aside from the attitudes they engender toward women, implicitly ask female readers who would understand the poem to read as if they were men. To understand the psychological discomfort that such reading practices entail for many women, heterosexual male readers would have to be required to read poems written in admiration of men's bodies or sexual parts. But, of course, few such poems are ever encountered in the course of a conventional canonical literary education.

The notion of the situated reader has its counterpart even in recent critical theories that would appear to continue to honor the authority of authors and texts. Indeed, in recent critical practice the figure of the author or what is sometimes referred to as "the author-function" (Gilbert, 1987) and the idea of the text are now generally seen as so situated that they nearly disappear into the context of the culture and the prevenient discourses that produce them. Thus, the author, as conceived by postmodern or poststructuralist critics, either disappears entirely (Barthes, 1968) or becomes less an originator of a text or source for an individual vision than a ventriloquist through whom a social class or culture speaks, less the one who writes than the one who is written upon by prior social and cultural forces. Similarly, where New Critics would speak of the integrity and discreteness of a literary text—its separability from all other texts (treating it like a person with an individual personality and identity—two concepts also called into question by modern theorists), postmodern critics emphasize the notion of intertextuality, the ways in which every text derives its meaning and its capacity to carry meaning from its relationship to a universe of other texts, including those that define its genre, those that it may be read in contrast to, those that make its language accessible to readers, those that teach us how to read it, and so on.

Operating on such conceptions of authors and texts, an influential group of critics known as the New Historicists (see Thomas, 1987) now tend to treat literary texts much the way anthropologists treat cultural artifacts—as pieces of a larger cultural mosaic. A professor of English with a New Historicist's orientation might teach Shakespeare's *Tempest* (as one of my colleagues actually did) not as an artistic monument or the achievement of an individual sensibility but as a cultural document in the discourse of colonialism—a text to be read in juxtaposition with accounts of voyages of discovery, colonial diaries, and slave narratives. Such a critic, moreover, would likely refuse to privilege the Shakespearean play over the less well known and nonliterary texts as a cultural document, arguing that our sense of Shakespeare's greater importance derives not from qualities that are inherent in the play but from culturally determined biases (based possibly on considerations of class, gender, or race) about what sorts of authors and texts deserve to be canonized as high art or literature.

Even those critics—most notably the deconstructionists—who seem most to resemble New Critics in their focus on the text itself and in their scrupulous attention to textual patterns and details ("close reading") have abandoned the New Critical faith in a literary text as a unified, discrete structure with a determinable and coherent meaning. They have declared, in contrast, that textual meaning is always undecidable in literary works and that, insofar as meaning can be apprehended at all, it is inevitably self-contradictory in its import. Where New Critics would once have found a determinate meaning successfully resolving whatever opposing thematic tensions might have been expressed in a work, deconstructionist critics (following the theory and example of such French writers as Roland Barthes and Jacques Derrida and such American theoreticians as J. Hillis Miller and the late Paul de Man) typically find a site for an unresolved contest between competing values, meanings, and even authorial voices (see Crowley, 1989).

The impulse of deconstructionists and other postmodern critics to demonstrate that texts are not the sites of unified numinous meanings but may be used to support competing ideologies or interpretive claims, that they speak not so much for genius authors but for larger cultural and political forces, and that their claim to privileged status is itself imposed by politically and economically determined cultural forces is all part of a movement among many poststructuralist critics to desanctify literature and challenge the hierarchy of values that privileges literary texts among the many textual discourses that people encounter in their daily lives. Such iconoclasm seems particularly central to the critical project of a school of British and American critics who engage in what is known as cultural studies or cultural criticism. Cultural critics (of whom the seminal theoreticians are Frederick Jameson, 1981, and the late Raymond Williams, 1979) have been among the most forceful exponents of the idea that literature has no inherent claim to superiority in cultural significance or human value over any other class of texts, including films, pop song lyrics, TV scripts, advertising copy, journalism, or technical writing. Cultural critics would ask those among us who continue to believe in the special power and value of literature to ask ourselves what authorizes our view of its superiority except cultural values that we subscribe to as members of a certain social class—the class that happens to control curriculum in schools.

While such a critical posture may seem to threaten the entire institution of literature and literary studies, it need not do so. To desanctify literature is not necessarily to dismiss it as an object of serious attention. On the contrary, it can be an invitation to us to admit other kinds of texts—including texts written by our students—for our equally serious attention. In other words, the effort of cultural criticism to disestablish literature as a privileged discourse is not an antiliterary impulse but a democratic one, urging us to broaden the range of texts to which we are willing to apply our interpretive and critical apparatus.

THE LITERATURE INSTITUTE FOR TEACHERS

• Goals and Methods •

The goal we proposed to the NEH for our Literature Institute for Teachers was to improve the teaching of literature in our region of California by faithfully replicating the National Writing Project model (Blau, 1988) for professional development, including the NWP model for conducting a summer institute, sustaining a professional community of "Fellows" through an ongoing follow-up program, and extending the influence of the professional community to other teachers through school-site inservice programs conducted by LIT teachers.

Faithful to the NWP model, our Summer Institutes in Literature were characterized by the following features:

- Four full weeks (twenty days) of full-day participation by all twenty-five participants

- Participants representing all grade levels from elementary school through university (our proportions were approximately 30 percent elementary, 50 percent secondary, and 20 percent tertiary—including community college, college, and university)

- Participants (all of whom had previous experience in a Writing Project summer institute) were selected for their expertise and experience as language arts teachers and their experience (or promise) as leaders for inservice programs for their colleagues. All were paid a $750 Fellowship stipend

- A commitment by all participants to read difficult literary texts together (and under the guidance of established scholarly authorities), to discuss problems and progress in making sense of those texts, and to write about the reading

- A presentation by each participant of an effective class-room-tested approach to teaching a literary text, using whenever possible one of the texts selected for the Summer Institute (these always included *Paradise Lost* and a Shakespearean play—*The Tempest* or *The Merchant of Venice*, and a children's novel, Lynne Reid Banks' *The Indian in the Cupboard*—plus additional works, which varied from year to year and included *Walden*, the poems of Emily Dickinson, Morrison's *Beloved*, stories by Zora

Neale Hurston, and Cisnero's *House on Mango Street*)

- Reading, supplemented by guest lecturers, on current literary theory and the major schools of criticism

Insofar as our first Summer Institute in Literature constituted an experiment in applying the Writing Project model to the teaching of literature, we initiated it with a number of concerns about its outcome. These can be stated as the questions we expected our experiment to answer:

(1) Would the teachers participating in our Institute find the experience as transformative for their teaching of literature as the Writing Project had been for their teaching of writing some years earlier?

(2) Could we build a collegial community through talking and writing about literature that would be as personally and professionally nourishing as the community of writers typically built in a Writing Project summer institute?

(3) Would small-group work be as effective as a model instructional method in the study of literature as it had been in the context of the Writing Project?

(4) Could our Institute yield for its participants the kind of new knowledge about literary theory and the study of literature that we hoped for without sacrificing the egalitarian model of staff development that characterizes the Writing Project? In other words, could the teachers learn new literary theory and critical methods as participants in a collegial community where their expertise as practitioners is as valued as the expertise of staff members and eminent visiting scholars?

To note that all of these questions were answered affirmatively by the end of our first summer and confirmed emphatically in our subsequent summers is not simply to say that we found the Writing

Project model for the professional development of teachers as valid for our work on the teaching of literature as it had been for our work on the teaching of writing. In fact, many of the participants reported that their work in the Literature Institute was even more transforming for them in terms of its impact on their teaching—that is, as measured by the degree to which it brought about changes in their classroom practices. But since all the teachers in our Literature Institute had completed an earlier Summer Institute in Composition and were already experienced as participants in collaborative groups and used to working in a collegial community, it may not be accurate to characterize our experiment as a test of the Writing Project model.

What our experiment did demonstrate that we didn't know in advance, however, was how powerfully the fundamental pedagogical principles that inform practice at virtually all Writing Project sites apply to the teaching of literature, or at least to the development of pedagogically satisfying and intellectually sound practices for the teaching of literature. I think it is likely that we would have learned similar lessons working with teachers who were not already experienced Writing Project teachers and expert teachers of writing, but I doubt if we would have made equal progress with a more inexperienced group of teachers or if we would have been nearly as able to frame our experiences in sound pedagogical principles or translate them so effectively into workable instructional strategies.

It is surely the case that the major crisis of our first Summer Institute in Literature (a crisis that might have suggested that certain essential Writing Project practices were not applicable to the study of literature) and our first important pedagogical discoveries may not have emerged with such a positive outcome so instructively among a group of teachers who lacked the experience and sophistication of Writing Project teachers in the teaching of writing and in the processes of sharing written work in small writing-response groups.

The story of that crisis and its resolution is, I think, emblematic of the pedagogical predicament that defines current standard practice in the teaching of literature—especially among language arts teachers who are well-informed and highly professional teachers of writing. It also reveals the theoretical and practical grounds for a solution.

• Reading Together:
A Social and Hermeneutic Crisis •

At the end of our first week of work as a community of teachers examining literary works (focusing largely on *The Tempest* and the beginning of *Paradise Lost*), several of the participating teachers complained that their work in small reading/writing groups wasn't enjoyable, as it had been in the Writing Project, and the consequence of their group work was that they felt themselves becoming less rather than more confident and competent in the exercise of their literacy. Many teachers noted, moreover, that in contrast to their experience in Writing Project writing-response groups, discussions in their small reading/writing groups were competitive rather than collaborative and led them to feel discounted rather than affirmed, ignored rather than heard, and alienated rather than affiliated in a collegial community.

The problem seemed to derive from what the teachers took as their obligation to arrive through their discussions in their reading groups at a "correct" or authoritative interpretation of the difficult texts they were studying. Although these same teachers had become fairly expert at responding to student papers and to each other's writing without posing an "ideal text" to which their responses directed the writer, their discourse on a literary text seemed to be directed to finding an ideal or right reading or at least a reading that satisfied their sense of what, according to New

Critical criteria, would constitute an adequate reading. Such a reading, they seemed to suppose, would discover the determinate meaning of the text and account for how that meaning was the product of the various strata of meaningful structures or features of the text (see Wellek and Warren, pp. 138–141). The test of correctness, of course, lay in the strength of the arguments that a reader could mount in defense of a particular reading or in the consistency of a reading with the readings provided by experts in critical introductions, guidebooks, or lectures. The nature of the discourse in the reading groups was therefore largely argumentative, competitive, and characterized by appeals to the authority of experts—appeals which appeared to discount the immediate reading experience of many members of the reading group.

To participate in a typical reading group with a number of English and language arts teachers is surely to make oneself vulnerable to a set of feelings quite opposite from those characteristically experienced by Writing Project teachers in small writing-response groups. In a writing-response group a writer is called upon to tell her own story or elaborate her own ideas. The auditors in the group who hear or read the written piece typically provide the writer with an account of what they understand the writer to be saying, what they can't understand, and what they might want to hear more about. Respondents typically encourage writers to tell more or clarify or experiment with other ways of getting across the story or idea that the writer seems to want to communicate. The focus of the discourse is on informing the writer on how each reader apprehends the written text so that the writer may reshape the text to achieve his or her own intentions (see Nystrand & Brandt, 1989). In a writing-response group, if you are the writer, then my discourse as a respondent is never competitive with yours. Rather it is designed to help you construct a meaning that is distinctively your own or over

• 35

which you are at least in control.

If we are colleagues in a reading group, on the other hand, and we subscribe to the view that there is a best or correct reading that our own readings must approximate, then unless our readings are alike, we will find ourselves competing for the same discursive space, making statements about a single text that, insofar as they disagree, appear mutually exclusive and in competition for the status of a correct reading. Moreover, whoever finds his own readings invalidated by the authority of normative or critically sanctioned readings must be tempted to doubt his capacity to arrive at a right reading—which is to say, to doubt the efficacy of his literacy. Such doubting is an invitation to literacy by proxy—to the kind of pseudo-literacy that is regularly practiced by student readers who characteristically make no attempt to understand texts for themselves but wait for a teacher or a guidebook to tell them what a competent reader is supposed to understand.

The problem we faced, then, as a community was first a social or interpersonal one: how could we work together in reading groups in a way that would produce the social and personal benefits that we had experienced in writing groups and that ultimately foster the development of more confident and competent writers (cf. Blau, 1987)? But it was also an intellectual and literary problem, for, finally, we could not value even the most mutually affirming techniques for working together on interpreting difficult literary texts if we could not regard the process and product of such group work as intellectually responsible. The challenge we faced, then, was one of finding a way, in the context of a reading group, to produce intellectually responsible readings of difficult literary texts while working together in a spirit of collaboration and mutual affirmation rather than competition and disconfirmation.

• Resolving the Social and Hermeneutic Crisis •

The first step toward solving our social problem was offered to us by Peter Elbow (1986) with the technique of methodological believing and doubting (*Embracing Contraries*, pp. 254–99), a method of encouraging more collaborative rather than competitive discourse between persons who take opposing views on any subject. The technique entails responding to a claim that you disagree with by first offering three reasons to support the position you oppose and then offering three reasons to oppose it. The real impact of the technique, however, in the context of our reading groups, derived from the power of believing. To try to support a literary interpretation that you initially oppose is to try to see a text from a perspective unlike your own, a perspective that often yields insights otherwise inaccessible to you. Moreover, your good faith effort to read a text from another reader's distinctive point of view (instead of arguing for your own) often frees the other reader from having to defend his position against yours, liberating him to see the defects in the arguments you are yourself trying to mount in support of his position. (Believing, of course, also becomes—and did become in our institute—a powerful epistemological and critical stance to take as a reader of a literary text, especially of a text like *Paradise Lost* where doubting is relatively easy, and offers the reader almost no opportunity to apprehend the perspective of the text).

The introduction of the technique of believing and doubting into the discourse of the reading groups in our Literature Institute offered the teachers an alternative to the competitive dynamic of argument, substituting for it a dynamic of collaboration, still initially in the form of an argument in which all participants became equally invested in all sides. More importantly, the readers within the reading groups found that the process of believing and the dynamic of collaboration offered them richer and more comprehensive readings of literary texts than they had access to before. Within a few days of first practicing methodological believing and doubting, most reading groups moved beyond the formal practice of the technique to group practices that were generally more dialogical than argumentative and more open to alternative and variant readings. Instead of competing for the same discursive space, members of reading groups found themselves collaborating to construct more inclusive readings or committing to a process of negotiation with each other and with texts that yielded multivoiced readings, which were valuable for the degree to which they revealed subtle features of texts at the same time that they reflected a range of plausible interpretive responses. If groups were prepared to argue for a best or most correct reading of a text, they looked for the interpretation that best captured the polyvocal conversation of the group itself.

With enough experience, most teachers found the composite reading, representing the voices and perspectives of all the readers in their group, more intellectually satisfying than any single normative reading or any authoritative reading available from a visiting specialist or critical text. On the other hand, many of the teachers also worried that any reading aside from a normative and authoritative one might have no real authority beyond the community of a reading group and might not therefore be sustainable in the wider literary community. From this perspective the collaborative approach to literary interpretation might seem acceptable in a Literature Institute for Teachers but not in classrooms where students are preparing for more advanced literary study and for examinations calling for conventional and authoritative readings (cf. McClelland & Blau, 1990, on standard practices in college prep classes).

Two responses presented themselves to this concern, one appealing to the authority of modern literary theory and the other appealing to the authority of the teachers' own experience as readers and interpreters in our Literature Institute and elsewhere. First, the theoretical challenges to New Criticism that have been launched in the past twenty years by such critical approaches as those of the reader-response critics and various poststructuralists have called into question the intellectual validity and authority of any meaning attributed to a literary text, so that the entire question of a determinate or correct meaning is at least problematic. Thus, teachers concerned with the intellectual value of the multiperspectived readings arrived at through collaboration would find as much or more theoretical justification for such readings as they would for more conventional and normative readings.

Second, the experience of the teachers in the Literature Institute in the first few days demonstrated to them firsthand (frequently reminding them of their experience in college literature courses) how the imposition of an authoritative reading undermines the capacity of the eccentric reader to exercise his own interpretive skill in the interest of making sense of literary texts. That is, instruction directed at achieving an authorized interpretation of a text may provide readers with literary knowledge in the sense that it offers them information on what constitutes a "right" reading, but insofar as it invalidates their own experience as readers, it disables their capacity to function as authentically literate persons. It will therefore be "false knowledge," precisely as Milton used that term—knowledge that opens their eyes but closes their minds. Students need not be deprived, however, of access to normative readings or the readings conventionally offered as authoritative, so long as these too are introduced with no more prior claim to credibility than any other reading. Just as it discounts the perceptions of students to impose any authoritative reading on them, so does it discount them as members of a larger community of readers to deprive them of readings that are well known and generally available to the literate community at large.

• Expanding the Repertoire of Reading and Teaching Practices •

The crisis in our reading groups in the first year of our Literature Institute for Teachers was resolved in a way that set a pattern for three years of Summer Institutes that characteristically exhibited a spirit of intellectual generosity and collaboration (punctuated by memorable debates and controversies, including a nearly destructive few days of "gender wars" ignited by intensive work on feminist issues: for an account of this experience, (see Armstrong, Smith, & Papoulis, 1990) in reading groups and in plenary sessions, with respect to variant and alternative readings of literary texts. Throughout the three summers, moreover, the most powerful continuing impetus toward hermeneutic generosity remained the intellectually and personally satisfying experience of the teachers who practiced it, even more than the force of any critical theory that might challenge New Critical presumptions or conventional practices. On the other hand, it is also the case that as teachers became familiar (through readings and presentations by guest consultants) with the alternative reading practices made available by recent critical theories—most especially by reader-response theory, feminist theory, and cultural criticism—they became increasingly inclined to offer strong readings that explicitly acknowledged their "situated" character and to recognize the intellectual legitimacy of a wide range of readings, including those that may have seemed "against the grain": that is, readings that explicitly resisted the values or cultural point of view that a work implicitly constructed as the shared culture of author and reader.

Out of such reading practices and the cumulatively developing critical sophistication of the teachers participating in our Literature Institute (LIT teachers) and in continuation meetings over the past several years, there has emerged a repertoire of teaching practices (most of which were demonstrated or employed experimentally in Summer Institutes) that are currently employed in the classrooms of many LIT teachers. These practices have gained wider currency from having been introduced more recently to large numbers of teachers at conferences and in staff development programs and inservice workshops conducted by LIT teachers. I want to describe a few of the most typical of those practices (some have been described in earlier articles by LIT teachers and staff members: see Dunstan, 1989; Roemer, 1989; Robertson, 1990) and suggest how they derive from or are supported by particular theoretical perspectives (not all of them literary) that extend our pedagogical vision beyond the familiar boundaries of conventional teaching practices and possibly beyond the constraints of what we think of (somewhat reductively, perhaps) as conventional New Critical doctrine.

Rereading Practices. A number of teaching practices that have become standard for LIT teachers in their classrooms and inservice workshops can be classified under the heading of rereading practices. Rereading would seem hardly to deserve recognition as an innovative teaching strategy, yet its importance to the reading process and to the acquisition of literacy is often not recognized in conventional curriculum planning. Rereading becomes particularly important, however, when literary instruction and the act of reading a literary text are reconceived, as they were in the Literature Institute, as versions of writing instruction or the act of producing a written text. Such a reconception of the reading process was fostered in the Literature Institute by theory and by reflection. That is to say, the experience of the teachers in the Literature Institute reflecting on their own layered processes of making sense of the difficult texts they were reading by rereading and gradually reconstructing their sense of the text revealed to them the degree to which they were engaged in a process that closely resembled the writing process and in which revision was an even more compelling and necessary move. Of course, their inclination to perceive their reading practices as a version of the writing process was surely a function of their familiarity with a large body of discourse about writing as a process and their introduction during the Institute to current theorized conceptions of reading as a matter of text construction.

To see reading as a process of vision and revision, moreover, is to acknowledge the status of early readings of a text (more dramatically than subsequent readings) as always provisional and very often partial or "mistaken," yet no more inadequate or symptomatic of illiteracy than a writer's rough and scratched out portions of a first draft are signs of the writer's incompetence or illiteracy. In fact, just as we have come to see the roughness and provisional character of a first draft as evidence of an emerging writer's competence (Calkins, 1979), so can students come to recognize that their own sense of puzzlement in their first reading of a difficult text is not a sign of their insufficiency as readers but part of the process that is experienced and endured by all competent readers when reading difficult texts.

Yet our experience in our Literature Institutes (and in observing classes) suggests that most teachers—and surely most students—are simply not aware of the degree to which reading difficult texts is a layered, onion-peeling (and sometimes tearful!) process, which in its initial stages can feel frustrating and daunting even to the most accomplished and literate readers (Blau, 1981). Hence, many of the teachers in our institute reported later that one of the ways that the institute influenced them most profoundly as readers (and subsequently as teachers) was in showing them that the puzzlement and frustration they often experience in their initial transactions with difficult literary texts are not signs of illiteracy or incompetence as readers, but reactions that come with the territory of trying to read many of the texts that are most worthwhile reading—worthwhile, in part, precisely because they enact structures of meaning that are unfamiliar and therefore difficult to grasp.

Composition theory and reading practice thus conspired in our Literature Institute to produce a model for literature instruction that gave a preeminent place to the notion of rereading or revision and yielded a number of teaching strategies that fostered rereading. Let me describe a few of those strategies now by presenting a typical sequence of instructional activities—a sequence I have witnessed in varying forms at virtually every grade level from the primary grades through teacher education classes.

The sequence typically begins with the introduction of a short literary text that students are asked to read to themselves, possibly making notes on what sentences, lines, or segments are most troublesome to them or possibly making entries in a double-entry journal as described by Berthoff (1981). Students are then asked to work in small groups or as a class and reread the text aloud by engaging in "jump in reading." This means that readers are free to "jump in" and read aloud, whenever a previous reader pauses to indicate the completion of a turn as reader. Students are free to read small or large segments of text but not to read so much that nothing is left for others to read. A paragraph or two would be a well-mannered "helping" with a short story. Besides one can always read again, later, if no one else jumps in.

The virtue of jump-in reading is that it allows students the freedom to read or decline to read without pressure from a teacher and to participate in a reading as members of a community of read-ers. Moreover, having already read the text once to themselves, they are less likely to read stumblingly as they try aloud to make plain syntactic sense out of what they are reading. Reluctant readers espe-cially appreciate jump-in reading because it allows them to avoid reading aloud, but also because it gives them the freedom to jump in when they feel ready. And they often gain confidence (and compe-tence) from hearing prior readers whose example teaches them how to pronounce unfamiliar words that may recur in a selection. I have observed even first graders, who are just learning to read, enjoying jump-in reading because it gave them a chance to read (sometimes with struggling pauses and sometimes aided by neighbors) their favorite parts of a story or a small segment of text that they felt they knew how to read. (For a particularly difficult short text—typically a lyric poem—students might be asked to read it a third time individ-ually or with a partner.)

Another rereading technique that is often employed after jump-in reading (punctuated first, perhaps, by some small group discussion identifying and addressing problematic lines or issues in the text and a return to the double-entry journals) is a technique known as "text rendering." Developed initially by a group of teach-ers working under Peter Elbow's direction at the Bard Institute for Writing and Thinking, text rendering is a version of what Elbow (1970) has called "pointing," in his instructions to students to respond to the writing of their peers by pointing to or saying back to the writer a short passage, sentence, phrase, or even a word that is particularly resonant or memorable for the reader or strikes the reader as particularly apt, interesting, or even puzzling.

In the context of literary study, text rendering entails reciting such passages from a text out loud for classmates to hear, and usual-ly to do so as the spirit moves the participants. Moreover, teachers typically encourage students not to feel preempted when another reader has called out a line that they had intended to render. Repetitions of portions of a text reveal something about the weight of meaning in particular passages and commonalities or contrasts in the responses of readers within a group (see Robertson, 1990).

In most secondary school or college classes these rereading activities would be followed by a related activity in which students would be asked to write interpretively about the text being read. A favorite activity in the LIT community of teachers is to have students at this point select from the text being studied any line, sentence, or phrase (possibly but not necessarily one that they heard read aloud in text rendering) that they regard as particularly important, interesting, or problematic. Then they are to write about it ("focused freewriting" as described by Belanof & Elbow, 1989; and Hammond, 1990; or a "quickwrite" is often called for here) for about ten minutes. Students are next instructed to read their writing in small groups (with selected pieces read to the whole class) and, finally, to report on the issues of interpretation, value, and response that emerge from the readings and small group conversation. Some teachers follow this activity with another writing activity, which asks students to discuss what their previous piece of writing reveals about them as "situated" readers—that is, as persons of a particular race, gender, class, social experience, sibling position, religious orientation, and so on.

Taken together, these two writing activities open up a range of responses to and interpretations of the assigned text and begin to look at how such responses and interpretations may reflect different reader perspectives. When students offer contradictory readings of a text they are also encouraged to practice Elbow's method of believing and doubting.

Other Changes in Teaching Practices and Expectations.

Other clusters of new teaching practices also characterize the methodological repertoires of the teachers who participated in our Literature Institutes. These include strategies for fostering hermeneutic generosity, numerous strategies for problematizing a reading (identifying questions and problems encountered in trying to make sense of a text—emphasizing the centrality of "re-vision" to the reading process); strategies for fostering collaboration and building a community of readers (in which a shared literary history fosters intertextual perspectives and shapes responses and interpretations); strategies for building fluency for students (expanding literary tastes, building confidence, promoting reading for pleasure, etc.); and strategies for exploring and shaping individual responses to and interpretations of texts.

Beyond extending their repertoire of teaching practices, participants in LIT reported changes in themselves and in their expectations as literature teachers that seem more fundamental than changes in methods and that underlie and account for methodological innovations. When asked to provide a series of statements (including some using the format of "I used to . . . , but now . . . ") to describe how their teaching changed as a consequence of their participation in the Literature Institute, virtually all of the teachers included at least one statement indicating that they had shifted the focus of authority in their literature classes from themselves and authoritative interpretations to the students' own constructions of meanings. As one teacher put it: "I used to think there were certain . . . right interpretations of texts that I had to teach my students, but now I see that 'making meaning' of texts is a more individual process and I need to . . . encourage my students to trust their own experiences and responses to texts." This same teacher notes that now she does "less teaching and more modeling" of her own processes as a reader. Other teachers echo these ideas: "I used to lead the students to the 'meaning' of the work, but now I allow all . . . the students' meanings to come forth in discussion." Another says, "I used to explain the meaning of difficult texts to students, but now I allow students to respond to texts from their own perspectives." And another: "I used to take more of an authoritative role in the classroom, but now I'm comfortable if the students take over." Another grants some authority to professional scholars but wants it shared by teachers and students: "I used to . . . rely on the views of authorities and not trust myself, but now I feel that my students and I are the authorities, willing to listen to published scholars but also . . . to trust ourselves."

This same theme of having moved, as some teachers themselves expressed it, "from a teacher-centered class to a student-centered class," recurs in slightly different terms in the responses of many teachers who speak of having learned to appreciate alternative responses to and interpretations of texts rather than becoming threatened by them. As one teacher put it: "I don't feel threatened; I feel challenged, nudged, surprised, uncertain, and sometimes hit in the face . . . but it's good. It's conversation." Along similar lines, many teachers mentioned that they "used to ask questions from the book" or direct discussion according to their own agenda, but now they "let students ask their own questions." Several teachers also mentioned a new awareness of the possibility of reading resistantly and of the value of acknowledging "situatedness" in readings—the possible influence of a reader's group membership by ethnicity, gender, class, and sociocultural experience. Noting a related change in their approach to reading, many teachers spoke of a new sense of responsibility for fostering in students a personal connection to literary works and for allowing students to write essays that reflect on and explore those connections. Some of these comments came from teachers who said, typically, that they "used to spend more time on imagery, theme, and structure" in teaching literary works.

Most teachers reported a new emphasis on rereading as part of the literary reading process and linking the teaching of literature to the teaching of writing in classes where they had formerly been treated as wholly separate enterprises. They also spoke of how they used to think of the act of reading literature as an isolating activity, but how they have now come to see it as a communal activity and an occasion for collaboration. In general, they became more willing to try new things, including a new willingness to introduce a greater variety of literary works into the curriculum—works that are not part of the traditional canon, particularly works by women and nonwhite authors.

Relations between theory and practice

The specific teaching activities I have described and the more general changes that took place in the teaching practices and expectations of the teachers who participated in our Literature Institute for Teachers suggest a complicated and interanimating relationship between a teacher's learning about current literary theory and changes in pedagogical practice. Although the changes I have reported in teachers' attitudes and practices seem to parallel some of the ways in which modern literary theory and critical practice have challenged the doctrines and practices of the New Criticism, it would hardly be accurate to say that the teachers who participated in our Institute were liberated from the constraints of an intellectually limited and pedagogically unsatisfying paradigm for literary instruction by a healthy dose of modern critical theory.

On the contrary, one of the most compelling forces for pedagogical change that teachers found during the Literature Institute was their own discomfort with New Critical practices as they tried to employ them in the context of the collaborative groups that they adopted from their Writing Project experience. That is to say, the teachers of the Literature Institute were persuaded to relinquish their allegiance to New Critical practices and notions about the need to establish an authoritative reading for a text not so much by newer literary theory as by the extreme social and intellectual discomfort they experienced in trying to employ New Critical practices in a collaborative context that they otherwise trusted pedagogically. The processes of believing and doubting and entertaining multiple readings, for example, were adopted as solutions to what was perceived as a pedagogical problem. Those solutions were then found to be sanctioned and supported by postmodern critical theory.

In this process of pedagogical transformation, literary theory still played a critical though secondary role. For one thing, literary theory conferred upon the teachers a sense of their efficacy by validating the uncertainties, the multiple readings, the resistances and the difficulties that they encountered in their transactions with literary texts and with each other, particularly by sanctioning personal or cultural responses and situated readings that teachers may have formerly felt constrained to suppress. Theory also relieved them of the academic responsibility they had thought to be theirs for leading students to the "correct" or authoritative readings of canonical texts. Pedagogical experiments in the Institute (and since then in classrooms) that invited a broader repertoire of responses to texts or encouraged readings from a wider range of perspectives were occasioned by the teachers' growing awareness of theory. Conversely, theory also served to sanction and refine a number of instructional practices that individual teachers had previously employed with great satisfaction in their own classrooms and demonstrated for their Institute colleagues—practices like creating dramatic improvisations to explore events in a literary work, inventing alternative endings, sharing personal experiences analogous to those in fiction, reading a poem from the point of view of its recipient or its subject, writing imitative texts, and so on.

Finally, it must be acknowledged that much of the theory that influenced and supported Literature Institute teachers in transforming their literature teaching practices in their own classrooms is not literary theory at all but composition theory and related theory in the areas of language acquisition and the social construction of knowledge (Krashen and Terrell, 1983; Hull, 1989). For aside from developing teaching strategies that were based on applying a writing process model of text construction to the process of construction meaning in reading, teachers participating in the Literature Institute were most profoundly influenced by current formulations about the ways in which writing is a process of construction meaning that takes place within the rich social and cultural context of a community of writers—precisely the sort of community of writers and readers that the Literature Institute teachers were constructing for themselves in their summer institutes.

Many of the instructional activities that have become distinctive marks of Literature Institute teachers in their classrooms—reading aloud, using collaborative reading and interpretation groups, attending to a variety of interpretive perspectives, and using various strategies to encourage hermeneutic generosity—are precisely those that help to establish and sustain a classroom culture or community in which authentic literary activity takes place and literary power is exercised in the service of socially valued goals. It is no accident that most of the inservice workshops that teachers from the Literature Institute now conduct at professional conferences and at school sites locally and nationally are announced under some variation of the title "Building a Literary Community in the Classroom."

REFERENCES

Armstrong, Smith, C., & Papoulis, I. (1990). Feminist awakenings in an NEH-funded literature institute for teachers. Paper presented at NCTE fall meeting in Atlanta.

Atwell, N. (1987). *In the Middle*. Portsmouth, NH: Heinemann

Barthes, R. (1968). The death of the author. In Dan Latimer (Ed.), (1989), *Contemporary critical theory*. New York: Harcourt Brace Jovanovich.

Berthoff, A. (1981). *The making of meaning*. Montclair, NJ: Boynton/Cook.

Blau, S. (1981). Literacy as a form of courage. *Journal of Reading, 25,* 101–106.

Blau, S. (1987). Contexts for competence in composition. *The Quarterly, 9* (Fall), 4–7+27. National Writing Project & Center for the Study of Writing: University of California, Berkeley.

Blau, S. (1988). Professional development and the revolution in teaching. *English Journal, 77,* 30–35.

Bleich, D. (1978). *Subjective criticism*. Baltimore: The Johns Hopkins University Press.

Brooks, C. (1947). *The well-wrought urn*. New York: Harcourt, Brace & Co.

Calkins, L. (1979). Andrea learns to make writing hard. *English Journal, 56* (May), 569–75.

Ciardi, J. (1959). *How does a poem mean*, Boston: Houghton Mifflin.

Crowley, S. (1989). *A teacher's introduction to deconstruction*. Urbana, IL: National Council of Teachers of English.

Dunstan, A. (1989). Building a literate community: Report from an NEH Literature Institute for Teachers. *The Quarterly, 11* (Summer), 10–14+27. National Writing Project & Center for the Study of Writing: University of California, Berkeley.

Elbow, P. (1970). *Writing without teachers*. New York: Oxford University Press.

Elbow, P. (1973). *Writing with power*. New York: Oxford University Press.

Elbow, P. (1986). *Embracing contraries: Explorations in learning and teaching*. New York: Oxford University Press.

Elbow, P. & Belanof, P. (1989). *A community of writers*. New York: Random House.

Fish, S. (1968). *Surprised by sin: The reader in Paradise Lost*. New Haven: Yale University Press.

Gilbert, P. (1987). Post reader-response: The deconstructive critique. In B. Corcoran & E. Emrys (Eds.), *Readers, texts, teachers*. Montclair, NJ: Boynton/Cook.

Graves, D. (1983). *Writing: Teachers and children at work*. Portsmouth, NH: Heinemann.

Hammond, L. (1991). Using focused freewriting to promote critical thinking. In P. Belanof, P. Elbow, & Fontaine (Eds.), *Nothing begins with an n: New investigations of freewriting*. Carbondale, IL: Southern Illinois University Press.

Hirsch, E.D. (1967). *Validity in interpretation.* Chicago: University of Chicago Press.

Hull, G. (1989). Research on writing: Building a cognitive and social understanding of composing. In *Toward the thinking curriculum: Current cognitive research.* Yearbook of the Association for Supervision and Curriculum Development.

Iser, W. (1978). *The act of reading: A theory of aesthetic response.* Baltimore: The Johns Hopkins University Press.

Jameson, F. (1981). *The political unconscious.* Ithaca: Cornell University Press.

Krashen, S., & Terrell, T. (1983). *The natural approach.* San Francisco: Alemany Press.

Langer, J. (1990). Understanding literature, *Language Arts, 67* (December), 812–816.

Lynn, S. (1990). A passage into critical theory. *College English, 52* (March), 258–71.

Marshall, J. (1989). *Patterns of discourse in classroom discussions of literature.* Albany, NY: Center for the Learning and Teaching of Literature.

McClelland, K. & Blau, S. (1990). *College preparatory vs. college reality: A study of the match and mismatch between college prep English classes and university freshman English classes.* South Coast Writing Project: University of California, Santa Barbara.

Moffett J. (1968). *Teaching the universe of discourse.* Boston: Houghton Mifflin.

Nystrand, M., & Brandt, D. (1989). Response to writing as a context for learning to write. In C. Anson (Ed.), *Writing and response: Theory, practice, and research.* Urbana, IL: National Council of Teachers of English.

Robertson, S. (1990). Text rendering: Beginning literary response. *English Journal, 79,* 80–84.

Roemer, M. (1989). Literate cultures: Multi-voiced classrooms. *The Quarterly, 11* (Jan), 10–13. National Writing Project & Center for the Study of Writing: University of California, Berkeley.

Rosenblatt, L. (1938). *Literature as exploration.* New York: Barnes and Noble.

Schweickart, P. (1986). Reading ourselves: Toward a feminist theory of reading. In E. Flynn and P. Schweickart (Eds.), *Gender and reading: Essays in readers, texts, and contexts,* pp.31–62. Baltimore: The Johns Hopkins University Press.

Thomas, B. (1987). The historical necessity for—and difficulties with—new historical analysis in introductory literature courses. *College English, 49,* 509–522.

Tompkins, J. (Ed.). (1980). *Reader-response criticism: From formalism to post-structuralism.* Baltimore: The Johns Hopkins University Press.

Wellek, R, & Warren, A. (1956). *Theory of literature.* New York: Harcourt, Brace & Co. (Original work published in 1949)

Williams, R. (1979). *Politics and letters.* London: New Left Books.

Wimsatt, W.K., with Beardsley, M. (1954). *The verbal icon: Studies in the meaning of poetry.* Lexington: University of Kentucky Press.

Zancanella, D. (1991). Teachers reading/readers teaching: Five teachers' personal approaches to literature and their teaching of literature. *Research in the Teaching of English, 25* (Feb), 5–32.

CHAPTER 3

BECOMING MEMBERS OF AN INTERPRETIVE COMMUNITY

Victoria Purcell-Gates
Harvard University

TODAY'S TEACHERS ARE STRUGGLING WITH the ways and means of facilitating literacy growth for their students through meaningful experiences with print in the classroom. "Meaningful print," for the most part, has been translated in many classrooms to mean literature. Thus, we are seeing the proliferation of "literature-based" classrooms, "literature-share" groups within whole language classrooms, and the inclusion of increasing amounts of children's literature in basal reading series.

Research and debate are focusing on the methods teachers use to facilitate children's ways of comprehending and responding to literature. These studies and discussions are often an attempt to bring together notions from both the reading comprehension and the literary response fields, two areas of inquiry from vastly different paradigms. Thus we see, on one end of the scale, work-books accompanying children's literature designed to teach vocabulary knowledge, main idea, and sequencing, and, at the other end, literature-response groups where children are encouraged to share their individual responses to pieces of literature within the context of a supportive group.

This paper contributes a developmental perspective to this study by looking at very young children on the verge of their formal schooling career. I suggest here that many young children begin school with the buds of literary response already in place, ready to bloom as they learn to read independently and thus experience literature for themselves. Accepting this, we can perhaps suggest fruitful ways for teachers of young children to encourage the development of this form of "readiness" for all children and to nurture its growth through classroom experiences.

LITERARY RESPONSE

Current literary response theories all specify a *construction* of meaning by the reader in response to the text. Meaning, in other words, does not reside solely in the text, to be discovered or "comprehended" by the reader. Meaning is the result of a process and is created during reading. Readers "make meaning," create understandings, construct wholes. Langer, in a recent study, (1989, 1990) describes the cognitive processes readers engage in as they construct meaning during reading of literary and nonliterary works. As a result of this study of thirty-six readers in grades 7 and 11, she describes varying stances readers take as they create and develop understandings of what they envision and an evolving whole during reading.

This process of constructing meaning through envisioning does not occur independently. The other player in this process is the text created by the author. Any discussion of reader/text by implication means reader/author. Readers construct meaning— develop envisionments—as interpretants of signs, the signs of the text (Morris, 1971). Rosenblatt (1978) describes the text as a blueprint, providing a plan without filling in all of the substance of the meaning (which Rosenblatt terms "the poem") created as the reader transacts with the text. Iser (1978) describes the role of the text in the reader/text relationship as providing access to what the reader is meant to visualize. His concept of the "implied reader" designates "a network of response-inviting structures, which will impel the reader to grasp the text" (pg. 34). These structures (of text), according to Iser, result from conscious manipulation of signs, and thus the response is elicited from the reader as interpretant of the signs. Thus, he goes on, syntax and semantics are generally presupposed in the pragmatics of signs, for these are implicit in the relation between the signs (text) and the interpretant (reader).

> The sentences themselves, as statements and assertions, serve to point the way toward what is to come, and this in turn is prestructured by the actual content of the sentences. In brief, the sentences set in motion a process that will lead to the formation of the aesthetic object as a correlative in the mind of the reader (pg. 110).

All of this leads us to the author, the creator of the text, the manipulator of signs. If readers construct meaning while reading literature by creating and developing evolving envisionments (Langer, 1989, 1990), then what role does the author play in this process? The creator of the text must provide the blueprint (or directions) for the creation of images, "response-inviting structures, which impel the reader to grasp the text," according to Iser (1978). The author must provide language for the reader to use in "the creation of a world" as Rader (1982) describes it. Novelists use precise, complex, and explicit language, according to Rader, to constrain the imaging of the reader. "Novelists work for explicit images, vivid details, well-chosen words whose connotations deepen and enrich their denotation, setting in motion the reader's imaginative processes of the novelists' choice" (p. 195).

A dynamic relationship results from this positioning of the author as the provider of particular types of signs for readers to interpret as they transact with the text to create meaning. This relationship depends upon a mutual understanding of the conventions of reader/text relationships. The author crafts text to provide for a particular interpretation or response by the reader. The reader responds to the text accordingly, given the same implicit understanding of these conventions. The reader and author are both members of the same interpretive community (Fish, 1980a).

• The Roots of Response •

In the section following, I will examine the relationship between reader and author as each relates to the reader/text relationship. I will look at it from a developmental perspective and present evidence suggesting an early acquisition of a *predisposition*, or readiness, for literary response by children. I contend that young children who have experienced and responded to literature by being read to by parents and others demonstrate their predisposition to literary response through evidence of their implicit understanding of the role of the author as a manipulator of signs.

Support for this claim comes from a study exploring the hypothesis that children who have been read to a great deal during the years prior to formal schooling learn "book language" (Holdaway, 1979). To test this, I presented preliterate kindergarten children, all of whom were "well read to"—children who had seen many books and heard them read as a frequent part of their growing-up experience—with two tasks intended to elicit two types of narrative, oral and written. I asked them to tell me all about their last birthday party, or a similarly salient event, and to pretend to read a wordless picture book to a pretend child (in the form of a toy). The book told a story in pictures of two characters (drawn as mice) who met adventures along a road to a castle where they explored, overcame hurdles in the forms of various scary events, and were rescued from the moat by a frog boatman.

I intended for the explicit direction "pretend to read" to activate their implicit register knowledge of written narrative, or "book language," if it existed. I wanted to isolate specific syntactic and lexical markers of a book language register in the children's speech. For this purpose, I presented them with two narrative tasks, one of which was associated more with oral language events (the "tell-me-about" personal narrative) and the other, which was associated more with written language events (the "pretend to read" from a book). Linguistic features from pretend readings were then compared to the personal narratives of a party or event in order to ascertain what linguistically, in terms of syntax and vocabulary, constituted this "book language" knowledge held by these children. Details of this study have been published (Purcell-Gates, 1988).

While analyzing the narratives for this initial study, I noticed features of the children's "pretend readings" that led me to a later analysis of the understandings of preliterate, often-read-to children. In that study, I explored the notion that these children evidence implicit understanding of the author's role in providing appropriate signs, or blueprints, to guide and constrain the response of the reader, an understanding seemingly too sophisticated for children at this age.

The participants in this study were twenty randomly selected kindergarten children, all of whom had been well read to. They came from the three elementary schools in a midsized school district in the urban San Francisco Bay Area. The children were representative of the population of the school district, which is racially mixed, middle to lower-middle class. Average age of the children was 5.6 years. They independently told me about a significant event in their lives (in most cases their birthday parties) and pretended to read from a wordless picture book.

I focused this analysis on lexical and syntactic features of the literary narratives (the pretend readings), which seemed to serve as blueprints for the visualizing or envisioning requested of the reader. Bear in mind that the children were asked to construct oral text that related the story revealed in the pictures of the wordless book. Their choices of syntactic and lexical items as they did this revealed insights into their implicit grasp of the author's role in the reader/text relationship.

The features discussed below as image-enhancing linguistic choices emerged in the original analysis, where they were found to be used significantly more often in the storybook narratives than in the personal narrations. The reader is directed to the published account of that study for details of that analysis (Purcell-Gates, 1988). The exception to this is the analysis on the imageability of the verbs used by the children. This will be described below in the section on verb choice.

• Response-Inviting Structures •

When the children pretended to read from a book to a pretend listener, they constructed image-producing and constraining text. They sounded fascinatingly close to the novelists described by Rader (1982) who "use precise, complex, and explicit language . . . for the reader to use in the creation of a world" (p. 195). They accomplished this through both their lexical and syntactic choices as they wove their stories. Here is a sample of one little girl's pretend-to-read story (see the appendix for transcription conventions; dots indicate length of pauses):

> There once . . . . was a brave knight, . . . and a beautiful lady. . . . . . they went . . . on a trip . . . . . a dangerous trip . . . . . . they saw a little castle. . . in the distance. . . . . they went to it. . . . . a mean . . . mean:n . . . mean:n . . hunter, . . was following them , . . . through the bushes. . . . at the entrance . . of the little castle. . . . . as he cree:ped out of the bushes, . . . he thought what to do. . . . . . as the drawbridge was opened, . . . they could easily get in, ... and the question was . . . . how to trick them, ... so . . . he waited. . . . . they started to go up, ... the path . . . of the drawbridge. . . . . . he slowly and quietly followed them. . . . .

Lexical Choices. One of the most salient features of the children's storybook texts were their lexical choices, as compared to their personal narrations. As they constructed their stories, they used words that painted pictures, clarified actions, specified images. Verb choice was especially apparent, probably because predicates are vital markers of narrative, relating events unfolding over time. In their book stories, the children used both a greater variety of lexical items for their predicates and ones judged significantly more image-provoking.

To measure the image-provoking strength of the verbs used by the children in their book stories, 111 college freshmen rated all verbs used by the children in their personal narrations and their pretend readings. The freshmen rated the verbs on one of five randomly ordered lists with the following 5-point scale:

> 0 = no imagery associated with this word
>
> 1 = imagery of marginal distinctiveness/ clarity/ specificity
>
> 2 = perceptible imagery of relatively low distinctiveness/ clarity/ specificity

3 = distinct/ clear/ specific imagery

4 = strongly distinctive/ clear/ specific imagery

A repeated-measures test (t) of the mean verb imageability ratings for each child's personal narrations and book stories revealed a significant difference ($p < .0005$) between the two, with the verbs used in the book stories judged to possess greater image-provoking power.

As the children constructed their story texts, they chose to portray action with such words as *crept, peeked, shivered, stumbled,* and *drag,* all choices that help readers envision the story with clarity and precision. This point is strengthened when one considers the types of verbs the children chose for their personal narrations: *come, got, played,* and *drove.*

Not only did the children choose verbs that were measurably more vivid and lively, they also varied their use of verbs to a greater degree when they assumed the role of creator of literary text. Type/token analysis revealed that the children used a significantly greater variety of verbs in their storybook renderings than they did when they related the personal event to the researcher ($p < .001$). This had the effect of producing a narrative of action, prototypical of the literary genre the children appeared to assign to the picture book—that of the fairy tale adventure. The perceptual effect on the reader of such text is to be held by it to a greater degree as the action not only quickly and continuously changes but is more highly specified. Following are sample narratives from one child. Comparing the two, one can see and actually feel the difference created by the more varied verb usage in the storybook narrative:

Personal Event Narrative:

. . . . and then after my party, ... we *had* like a little . . . family party, . . . and . . we *went* . . . the San Francisco Zoo. . . . 'cause I *got to choose* where to go, ... and I *said* "San Francisco Zoo." . . . well, . . my grandma *was* there, . . . gramma *flew* all the way from South Dakota . . . . except for then she *lived* . . . . a-actually . . .

Aberdeen, South Dakota, but . . sh . . then she *lived* on the coast. . . . . except for now she *lives* . . back back back. . . . . and we even *drove* to her house. . . . and we *dro:ve* down. . . . . and, . . . we *saw* the lio:ns, . . .

Storybook Narrative:

. . . . the young lady *was* afraid *to go* any farther. . . . . but the young knight, ... *tried to drag* her away. bats . . . *is* what they *were*. . . . bats, ... spooky /babyh/ bats. . . . . . the knight . . . *laughed* . . . /?/ and *laughed* more. . . . . . . they *went* up another stairway. . . . and another spook . . *hit* the ground. . . . a big . . blue . . ragged . . monster. . . . coming out . . and out. . . . . it *came* all the way out, ... and then with his stick, . . . he finally *got* it /?/. . . . . . . they *saw* a light. . . . . they *stuffed* the bag . . out the window. . . . . and *pushed* her out. . . . . she *fell* . . kersplash. . . . . into the pond. . . . . a nice frog *was rowing*.

Aside from verb usage, the children employed other lexical means to achieve text that "created a world" for the reader. These included use of *-ly* adverbs, sound effects, and direct quotes.

The *-ly* adverbs appears to be a particular marker of written story narrative (Cook-Gumperz, 1986, personal communication). Their communicative effect is to more fully specify action, thus providing guidance for the reader in the envisioning process. The child whose storybook text appears above, for example, composed, "he *slowly* and *quietly* followed them." The reader of such text can create a much more specific and image from this than would be possible without the *-ly* adverbs. While not all children included *-ly* adverbs in their story narratives, their overall frequency as compared to the personal experience narrative was statistically significant $(p < .02)$.

Almost all of the children inserted sound effects into their stories, resulting in increased imagery for the reader. *Kasplash! Sklunk! Roar! Poof! Spla:asssh!* Terms like these injected aural imagery into the stories to further bring them to life. Sound effects are loved by children of this age and were also used in their personal narratives. However, they were used significantly more often in the literary narratives ($p < .01$).

The use of direct quotes also served to enliven and sharpen the imagery called forth by the story narratives. As with the sound effects, the result of the use of direct quotes is to round out the perceptual landscape with indicators for aural images. While in their personal narratives, the children tended to relate the occurrence of speech indirectly (" . . . my stepdad was telling us . . . what was down there"), they all included direct quotes in their story narratives:

> . . . . she said, ... "see?" . . . . "see?" . . . and they said, . . "we did it," . . "great," . . and the prince said, . . "come on." . . . . Frog said, "bye bye," . . . . "Ooo" Noscza said, . . . "that is haunted," . . . she whispered . . he said, . . to himself, . . . "what's this dumb stuff doing in the castle?" . . . and they all shouted, "hooray" and went home.

Syntactic Choices. In the original analysis of this data, a number of syntactic features were identified that were used significantly more often in the storybook narratives than in the oral personal narratives ($p < .02$). These were referred to as Literary Word Orders. Seen through the lens of the present analysis, these features appear to serve pragmatically to guide and constrain the imaging of the reader. It appeared that the children implicitly ordered and reordered within phrases, clauses, and sentences to guide the reader's evolving envisionments.

Consider the following example of syntactic order:

> . . . as the two men rowed, the dripping lady was in between.

Two types of syntactic features that differentiated between the narratives produced by the children can be seen in this example.

The first is the preposed adverbial, *as the two men rowed,* and the second is the attributive adjective, *dripping.* These two features, representing syntactic choices or constructions, were used frequently by the children when they created the literary texts. They are also very typical of published literary text. By preposing the adverbial, the author can direct the reader's evolving concept more specifically, setting conditions for the image before the reader can go astray with an idiosyncratic one.

The same argument holds for the choice of an adjective of attribution rather than one of state ("The *dripping* lady" as opposed to "The lady was *dripping.*"). Chafe and Danielewicz have shown (1982, 1986) that the use of attributive adjectives is a marker of written text as compared to oral, reflecting the greater syntactic integration of writing. From a pragmatics viewpoint, the use of attributive adjectives can also be seen as a device to provide clear and specific guideposts for the reader as meaning is constructed.

Additional types of syntactic orderings in the children's storybook texts appeared to reflect the author's role in providing "impelling structures" for the reader to use for the creation of clear and specific images. These included subject/complement inversions, inserted adverbials, and subject/verb inversion. Following are examples from the children's pretend readings that include these syntactic reorderings. Reading them, one can sense how they serve to help the reader envision clearly what the author intends:

> . . . behind them were dark, dark eyes. . . . . as he creeped out of the bushes, he thought what to do . . . he slowly and quietly followed them. . . bats . . is what they were, . . . so they went a little close to the yellow ey:es . . . . slowly, . . they went up the stairs. . . but quietly, Mrs. . . . Mice . . . whispered, ... they heard a . . . . big . . voice. . . . . in the dark dark . . . . uh . . . cage. . . but . . . a evil villain was behind them.

The following is my favorite example of syntactic manipulation. This little boy took my injunction to "make it sound like a book story" to heart and produced a lengthy story text. This example is my favorite because it shows a young child who can neither read nor write independently visibly (or audibly, as the case may be) struggling to control some of the linguistic conventions of literary text. Through his attempts, repairs, abandonments of clauses, and so on, he gives us observable data supporting the notion that children this young know on some subconscious level that story text involves particular syntactic and lexical choices:

> . . . he tried to go quickly, but . . . also quietly. . . . he said, ... said Mr. and Mrs. Mice, ... didn't even say a wor:d. . . . . . but Mrs. Mice knew that someone had been in there, . . 'n trying not to disturb Mr. Mice, . . . who didn't believe. . . . . . suddenly, . . . they saw some . . . . yellow . . eyes.

The data presented here fit most closely, I believe, with Fish's (1980a) notion of an interpretive community where all members (readers and authors) learn through social and cultural involvement the conventions that enable them to create, identify, and respond to literature.

Fish (1980a) describes the shared knowledge among the members of this interpretive community as tacit knowledge and asserts that it is *knowledge* in the sense that it is acquired through participation in the community. That knowledge is social as well as conventional and informs both the author as creator of text and the reader as interpreter of text.

Interpretation of the data presented here requires an assumption of tacit knowledge since these children were all too young to hold conscious control over the vocabulary and syntactical choices that indicate such linguistic sophistication. Rather, they showed evidence of their membership in an interpretive community by their response to the directive to "pretend to read" from a book and to "make it sound like a book story." All of these children were selected for this study because they had been extensively read to during their younger years. This assured their membership in the community of literature—in the interpretive community. While the purpose of the study was not to establish a causal relationship between types of linguistic knowledge, or control, and the activity of being read to, suffice it to say that as part of a later study, a group of children who had not been read to performed in predictably different ways on this same "pretend reading" task (Purcell-Gates & Dahl, 1991). Thus, Fish's notion of an interpretive community with which tacit knowledge is acquired through social and conventional means is established.

These data present very young children who seem to implicitly understand that the role of literary text is to provide guidance and constraint of imaging. Their lexical and syntactic choices as they constructed literary text for their "pretend readers" demonstrated in measurable ways that they "knew" the authorial role and apparently "knew" this from having assumed the reader, or interpretant, role for so long. Thus they appear to instantiate Fish's (1980b) and Rosenblatt's (1978) assertion that one cannot separate reader and author. The reader is the author and the author is the reader; readers write texts, according to Fish. From this data, we glimpse the very beginnings of this state.

One can also refer to the tacit knowledge demonstrated by the children in this study as Culler (1975) does in terms of "literary competence." He defines literary competence as the "implicit understanding of the operations of literary discourse that tells one what to look for" (p. 114). Again, we see the isomorphism between the author and the reader in this portrayal of the reader/text relationship. *Competence*, as a term, though, often connotes "skill," especially to individuals involved in the schooling of young people. *Skill*, as a term, tends to lead educators in search of ways to inculcate a conscious acquisition of that skill. In the case of literature, this has for the most part led to the *teaching* of "those operations of literary discourse that tells one what to look for." Thus, the focus, in most classrooms today, is on the *text*, as an object, a situation that is an almost complete perversion of that described by Fish where tacit knowledge is acquired in social and conventional ways as members participate in an interpretive community. The goal of these two learning situations is the same, but the process for reaching that goal could not be more different. The description in this paper of children who have apparently acquired this literary competence in ways similar to those described by Fish contributes to the discussion. By implication, we can assert that the most effective way to facilitate literary competence in children and young adults is to involve them as true participants in an interpretive community where, through meaningful and intentional response to literature, they acquire the knowledge of the reader-author/author-reader relationship that defines this community.

PROVIDING AN INTERPRETIVE COMMUNITY IN THE CLASSROOM

While many children begin kindergarten and first grade as full members of an interpretive community, as demonstrated above, many others do not. Children who have not participated in story reading events have not had the opportunities to acquire implicitly the interpretive conventions they will need to respond to and learn from literary texts as they progress through school. It seems apparent, then, that one essential role of the teacher of young children is to provide them with this opportunity within the context of the classroom.

The injunction that kindergarten and first grade teachers read stories and books to children is not new. However, all too often this event is seen as superfluous to academic priorities whenever "back to basics" movements or increased community pressure for higher test scores arise. The research presented here and elsewhere (Pappas, 1988; Purcell-Gates, 1988; Snow, 1983; Sulzby, 1985; Teale, 1986) all strongly suggests, though, that the implicit knowledge children acquire from participating in many and varied story reading events underlies and supports the later development of skills in reading and writing that constitute many of the "basics" and emerge in the form of high test scores.

Story reading in the classroom, if its rationale is to provide experience in an interpretive community, must become an integral and contextualized aspect of the classroom. By this I mean that just reading *to* a whole-class group of children once a day does not recreate the experience enjoyed by the many children who have been "well read to" in their homes and communities during the years preceding schooling. The term *community* implies a group of people living in the same locality or with common interests. Criteria for being "well-read-to" are based on story-reading events that include such aspects as (1) choice (of story as well as when that event will occur); (2) frequency; and (3) opportunities for spontaneous response and give-and-take between reader and listener. All of these factors reflect "community," where all members are actively involved in the ways in which events unfold. These underlying rules of community are violated when one member (the teacher) controls the event and reads *to* other members rather than *with* them.

Let me describe some classrooms where I believe true interpretive communities are being created. In one kindergarten class, during a large block of "choice" time, children are encouraged to choose a book either individually or as a small group and ask a parent volunteer to sit with them and read. Parents and the teacher can be seen in hallways and nooks, on rugs and in chairs, reading to and with young children. The children often snuggle close or climb in laps in recreations of the "lapreading" events described in the literature about parent/child storyreading. Very seldom do the children request only one story at a time; usually they go back and forth from reader to shelf as books are finished and new ones chosen.

In another classroom, "transition" times are used for story-readings. Again, parent volunteers are encouraged to be present during before-school times, preceding and following recess times, and just before the end of the school day. Children are encouraged to choose stories and request reading-together times with the volunteers as they wait for the bell to ring or the teacher to call the class together for whole-group lessons.

In both of these instances, one can see recreations of home story-reading events: children initiate the activity and participate in the selection of the material; children have the opportunity to hear and respond to many instances of literary text; and—because of the intimacy resulting from the individual or small group nature of the events, real, spontaneous response both by the listener and by the reader is facilitated.

Classrooms such as those just described provide children, many for the first time, opportunities to assume membership in an interpretive community. As such, they learn in deep and implicit ways the conventions of response to literature that will enable them to acquire the skills needed to understand and enjoy literature as well as to write their own literary texts. While research is discovering that many children acquire these foundations through home reading events, we are also aware that many others do not. Those who do not are often the children who fail to benefit from formal literacy instruction. I suggest that, for these children, we must attend very seriously to the beginnings of the process and work to ensure that they are given the opportunity to develop the implicit knowledge that marks one a full member of an interpretive, literate community.

REFERENCES

Chafe, W. (1982). Integration and involvement in speaking, writing, and oral literature. In D. Tannen (Ed.), *Spoken and written language: Exploring orality and literacy.*
Vol. IX of Advances in discourse processes. Norwood, NJ: Ablex.

Chafe, W., & Danielewicz, J. (1986). Properties of spoken and written language.
In R. Horowitz & S.J. Samuels (Eds.), *Comprehending oral and written language.*
New York: Academic Press.

Cook-Gumperz, J. (1986). Personal communication. Berkeley, CA.

Culler, J. (1975). *Structuralist poetics.* Ithaca, NY: Cornell University Press.

Fish, S. (1980a). *Is there a text in this class? The authority of interpretive communities.*
Cambridge, MA: Harvard University Press.

Fish, S. (1980b). Literature in the reader: Affective stylistics. In J.P. Tompkins (Ed.),
Reader-response criticism (pp. 70–100). Baltimore: The Johns Hopkins
University Press.

Holdaway, D. (1979). *The foundations of literacy.* Auckland, New Zealand: Heinemann.

Iser, W. (1978). *The act of reading: A theory of aesthetic response.* Baltimore: The
Johns Hopkins University Press.

Langer, J. (1989). *The process of understanding literature.* (Report Series 2.1).
Albany, NY: Center for the Learning and Teaching of Literature.

Langer, J. (1990). The process of understanding: Reading for literary and informative purposes. *Research in the Teaching of English, 24,* 119–160.

Morris, C. (1971). *Writings on the general theory of signs.* The Hague.

Pappas, C. (1988). The development of children's sense of the written story register: An analysis of the texture of kindergarteners' "pretend reading" texts.
Linguistics and Education, 1, 45–80.

Purcell-Gates, V. (1988). Lexical and syntactic knowledge of written narrative
held by well-read-to kindergartners and second graders. *Research in the
Teaching of English, 22,* 128–160.

Purcell-Gates, V., & Dahl, K. (1991). Low SES children's success and failure at early
literacy learning in skills-based classrooms. *JRB: A Journal of Literacy, 23,* 235–253.

Rader, M. (1982). Context in written language: The case of imaginative fiction. In
D. Tanned (Ed.), *Spoken and written language: Exploring orality and literacy.*
Norwood, NJ: Ablex.

Rosenblatt, L. (1978). *The reader, the text, the poem.* Carbondale, IL: Southern
Illinois University Press.

Snow, C. (1983). Literacy and language: Relationships during the preschool years. *Harvard Educational Review, 53*, 165–189.

Sulzby, E. (1985). Children's emergent reading of favorite storybooks: A developmental study. *Reading Research Quarterly, 20*, 458–481.

Teale, W. (1986). Home background and young children's literacy development. In W.H. Teale & E. Sulzby (Eds.), *Emergent literacy: Writing and reading* (pp. 173–206). Norwood, NJ: Ablex.

Tompkins, J.P. (1980). An introduction to reader-response criticism. In J.P. Tompkins (Ed.), *Reader-response criticism* (pp. ix–xxvi). Baltimore: The Johns Hopkins University Press.

CHAPTER 4

FROM LITERATURE TO LITERACY: A NEW DIRECTION FOR YOUNG LEARNERS

Nancy L. Roser
University of Texas at Austin

MORE THAN FIVE THOUSAND CHILDREN'S books are published each year in the United States. In just one six-month period, over five hundred new picture books arrived in the offices of *The Horn Book* (Silvey, 1990). There is a greater possibility of locating good literature for children today than at any point in history. And just in time. Across the country, interest in children's literature continues to escalate, accompanied by a fervent belief in the value of literature in classrooms—from the very beginning of schooling. Teachers, perhaps more familiar and comfortable with children's literature than ever before, are increasingly intolerant of "textbook text"—prose created to conform to prescriptive criteria and intended to be instructive to children's literacy but not necessarily to awaken them to reasons for becoming literate. Either causally or contiguously, literature in classrooms waxes while reliance on artificially constructed texts wanes.

But what does this watershed signal for literacy instruction? What is to prevent entrenched notions of "teaching to read/teaching to write" from impinging on books written, illustrated, and designed expressly for aesthetic transactions? What part can reader-response theory play in kindergarten and first grade curricula already overstuffed with ensuring the foundations of children's achievement in everything, including letters, sounds, and growth toward conventional literacy? If literacy teaching and learning are supported solely by quality trade books, what will become of such mainstays as code instruction, practice opportunities, and even teaching dependable words to master? If access to "shallow-water" text is reduced, and young literacy learners dive immediately into "real" books (the best of which were not created to teach them to read), what is to keep the least able from drowning?

To borrow Langer's term (this volume), some answers may depend upon a new "envisionment" of literacy teaching and learning: The task becomes not so much one of teaching literacy so that children can reach for literature but rather one of offering literature so that children *will* reach for literacy. This chapter addresses some of the challenges teachers of young children will meet in the next decade as they work toward teaching literacy from this somewhat different direction. The teachers addressed are those who have soberly accepted the responsibility of teaching children to read and write, ever cognizant of the limited instructional time to accomplish their preeminent task; their students are those whom Purcell-Gates (this volume) credits with having "the buds of literary response [and much more] already in place," even though they have not yet begun to read conventionally. The following issues organize the discussion:

- the role of literature in the beginning literacy program
- the role of the teacher/guide to literature

- the role of the teacher/guide to literacy
- avoiding the hazards of the trail

THE ROLE OF LITERATURE IN THE BEGINNING READING PROGRAM

Long ago, there was no question as to the relation of literature to literacy—the link was secure. Yet it was adult literature that served as the tool of literacy instruction, as well as a means of conserving religious, moral, and patriotic values (Smith, 1986; Venezky, 1987). As the *teaching* of reading began to claim a scientific base, more specialized materials were created, offering beginning readers both didactic text and vocabulary controls. Over time, these contrived materials have incited strong negative reaction in a professional community critical (to varying degrees) of the materials' sterility, word-centeredness, controlled language, and absence of multicultural literature as well as the pseudo-scientific nature of instructional prescriptions and sequences (Brennan, Bridge, & Winograd, 1986; Hunt, 1969; Jensen & Roser, 1987; Moir & Curtis, 1968; Newton, 1967; Roser, 1987; Russavage, Lorton, & Millham, 1985; Shannon, 1987).

Teacher education, as judged by textbooks written for teachers, also became absorbed in the research movement that tended to separate the teaching of literacy from the teaching of literature. Beginning about 1920, teacher education texts addressed themselves to a much greater degree to *how to teach* and were much less concerned with *what to read* (Martinez & Roser, 1982). Even with the onset of widespread literature initiatives (California Department of Education, 1987; Cullinan, 1989), some remnants of that separation phase remain. For example, in some universities, courses in children's literature are still completely distinct from courses in reading/language arts; as a result, in some classrooms, sight word recognition and mastery of sound/symbol patterns still serve as gate-keepers to children's literature and to opportunities to write and read. Also understandable is the observation that some teachers of beginners are not as knowledgeable as they would like to be about how to rely on literature to teach literacy.

By enlarging texts (using "Big Books"), Holdaway (1979) offered a methodology for teaching literacy through literature, capturing an instructional intimacy akin to an individual storytime experience yet providing an entire group of children with visual access to the print. Still, are all books that can be enlarged for instruction to be considered "literature"? My own first grade teacher, for example, used enlarged preprimers on chart stands so that all of us could be involved in "corporate" rather than competitive learning, as Holdaway describes the shared reading that children do with Big Books. The difference is, of course, that our Dick and Jane was not as inherently satisfying or meaningful as a story that can be "lived" through, such as *The Very Hungry Caterpillar* (Carle, 1979), or as rhythmical and rollicking as *Chicka Chicka Boom Boom* (Martin, Jr. & Archambault, 1989) or as instantly mastered as *It Looked Like Spilt Milk* (Shaw, 1947).

Unarguably, the emerging reader, like his middle- and upper-grade schoolmates, deserves a rich supply of the very best of written language as core to literacy-learning. Besides the opportunity to hear and read good books because of the richness of the language models, children need literature because good stories help them to make sense of the world, educate the imagination, feed the desire to read, challenge the intellect, and deepen the awareness of self and others (Cullinan, 1987). Fortunately, good literature also supports literacy achievement (See Tunnell & Jacobs, 1989, for a review).

For literature to seep or step or surge into classrooms (and then prevail there as support for the beginning literacy program), some safeguards should be considered. First, as alluded to earlier, teachers and those who serve teachers (administrators, supervisors, media center personnel, and teachers of teachers) must know and be able to recommend and supply a wide variety of books to children. Books in the classroom must be, as Hickman (1983) asserts, not merely accessible but unavoidable. Books propped next to the gerbil cage, aligning the chalk ledge, and commanding the science, art, and writing centers announce their invitations to emerging readers. Stories worth talking about, poems worth hearing again, and well-crafted informative texts are part of the literature experience. When a wealth of books of all types are read to children, reread, laughed about, talked about, inspected, referred to, written about, enacted, and read yet again, literacy gains its surest foothold.

But, particularly for young children, the supply of literature in the classroom must include another kind of text: predictable books. These repeatable, chantable, invitational, almost instantly readable books include patterned texts of all types—rhyming, rhythmic, repetitive, give-away texts that children instantly participate in. These predictable texts (the decision as to which are "literature" and which are not won't be definitively settled here) help to secure the link between oral and written language and to support successful "reading" along and reading alone from the very beginning. Decidedly, predictable text is enjoying a marketplace, available to teachers and parents in quantities unparalleled in children's book publishing. And, although predictable texts may not be the meatiest books for chewing over in class discussions, they are quite digestible for learning to read.

In addition to teachers knowing books, keeping informed about the range of literature for children, and supplying both meaty and digestible books for beginners, a second safeguard needs to prevail in literature-based classrooms: We must learn to be protective of literature in the classroom. As Babbitt (1990) warned, "fiction is a fragile medium. A good story can collapse if it's made to bear too much weight" (p. 696). Good stories can be crushed in kindergartens as surely as in high school English classes. Stories and texts in both places must have a chance to be experienced first as works of art (Cianciolo, 1982). Attention to print, to the author's or illustrator's craft, to the "messages" of literature—or to any other of the myriad ways in which stories are scrutinized—should be part of subsequent visits to text. Literature is not primarily an instructional tool, so in classrooms, as in life, it should exist first for its own sake. When it does become a vehicle for learning, the teacher/guide must be knowledgeable about what is to be learned as well as when, why, and how.

THE ROLE OF THE TEACHER AS GUIDE TO LITERATURE

Eeds and Peterson (1991) compared the teacher's role as guide through literature to the task of being a museum curator—lending one's own experience and insights (eyes and thoughts and feelings) to novices—parcelled in sensitive doses. I like that metaphor. Teachers as curators first invite children to see, think, or feel in their own ways in response to stories but eventually nudge them beyond their initial responses toward literary insights and aesthetic judgments. Nudges are not ideas imposed from above but rather encouragement to return to the story to find a base for particular interpretations and judgments (Rosenblatt, 1938, 1983). Curators encourage the rethinking of one's own personal experiences that connect with the art form; they give the language of the medium to the spectators so that they, too, can become active participants.

Cianciolo (citing Miller, 1981) suggests that when literature is shared in the classroom it can be experienced as an *event*, as an *object*, and as a *message*. Story as *event* involves an internal, aesthetic response to the story as a lived-through experience. For example, students in Linda Cullinane's first grade had intense, personal involvement with *Oliver Button Is a Sissy* (de Paola, 1979) and with *Ira Sleeps Over* (Waber, 1972). The books challenged thinking about gender and age/behavior stereotypes, and the children had plenty to think about and issues to raise:

> "It's both (books) about a boy who liked to do girl
> things."

> "I think it's meanly."

> "If they laughed at me, I'd go over there and kick their
> butts off."

> "I wonder who was the one that changed the words on
> the school wall."

Afterwards, Rachel wrote in her journal: "I WUDER WiY OLIVER BUTTON wit pla with The UVr Bovs. [I wonder why Oliver Button wouldn't play with the other boys]." As in many good literature discussions, the role of the teacher was not one to settle issues but to help gain hearing for them.

Similarly, when Mr. Becker read his first graders the 1992 Newbery winner, *Shiloh* (Naylor, 1991), the children's first responses were to the story as an *event*. *Shiloh* is a story set in West Virginia of a boy-dog bond that is immediate and unshakable. Like Ms. Cullinane's class, Mr. Becker's students talked a great deal about the story. They wanted to tell what *they* would do if they found a mistreated dog; they described the courage and compassion that Marty showed; and they pondered from their levels of experience whether doing something wrong (like hiding a dog that isn't yours) is ever right.

When story is considered *as object*, readers think and talk about how the story works, how it is crafted by the author/illustrator, how, for example, characters grow and change or how mood is established. For example, from a kindergartner: "Did you notice how in Jack Kent's books things start out small, then get big, then get small again?"

But the line between considering literature as objective and literature as literature is really an invisible one. Certainly, no serial progression is intended in children's awareness of the literary craft. Sometimes, though, it is the teacher who signals that those observations are also the way readers talk about books: "I was thinking," Mr. Becker said quietly, "that Phyllis Naylor made this story (*Shiloh*) as soft as a beagle's ear in some places, and as prickly as a cocklebur in others." And twenty-six first graders were made aware that an author had deliberately chosen her words to help them feel a wiggly, warm dog and the danger he faced. Mr. Becker didn't use the literary term *mood* in the discussion that day, but some of his children (who hadn't done so before) began to reach for an understanding that a story is crafted.

The illustrator's contribution is also part of the craft to be considered when story is viewed as object. Young children who are led to be more visually literate appreciate and are knowledgeable of the art and artistry in their books. Arguing for more publisher-provided information within picture books about the techniques of the art itself, Silvey (1990) asks,

> If we want to use the magnificent art in picture books to full advantage, if we want our children to become visually literate as well as computer literate, then more information needs to be given to those using the book. What better way to teach children the difference between watercolors and oil paintings than in a storybook they love? (p. 132)

When story is construed and talked about as *message*, children focus on the lessons characters learn, consider the themes and multiple meanings of the story, and speculate about author intentions. Susan Lehr (1988, 1990) showed that very young children can talk about themes when the works are within their reach, when the invitations are extended, and when there is time for receiving the responses.

Accepting the responsibility for being literature teachers means sharing with beginners the keys to becoming literate thinkers. It involves knowing how to select good books for children, how to read them for their essence, how to engage children in conversations about books, how to help them gain confidence in relying on text to support their ideas, how to guide literature study with young children, how to provide them opportunities for responding in myriad ways, and how to listen, really listen, for the results.

• Guiding Storytime •

Researchers who have investigated factors that appear to contribute to children's successful literacy acquisition point again and again to the significance of the hours the children have been read to (Adams, 1990; Cochran-Smith, 1983; Durkin, 1966; McCormick, 1977; Teale, 1984; Wells, 1986). In our research with teachers and children during storytime across south Texas (See Roser, Hoffman, & Farest, 1990, for a description), my colleagues and I have explored such issues as the influence of storytime experiences on children's story talk (Roser & Hoffman, 1992), on their literacy growth, attitudes, and book familiarity (Hoffman et. al., 1991), on teachers' story sharing strategies (Hoffman, Roser, & Farest, 1988; Roser & Martinez, 1985), and on the curricular shifts that occur when storytime becomes a planned event (Hoffman, Roser, Battle, Farest, & Isaacs, 1990). Other investigators, too (e.g., Cochran-Smith, 1984; Feitelson, Kita, & Goldstein, 1986; Green & Harker, 1982; Martinez & Teale, 1989; Mason, Peterman, & Kerr, 1989; Morrow, 1984, 1988; Morrow, O'Connor, & Smith, 1990; Teale, Martinez, & Glass, 1989), have described classroom storytime events, examined the effects on comprehension or achievement, analyzed teachers' story-book reading styles, and addressed the adults' role in promoting response. Regardless of the confluence or distinction of their research lines, all of these investigators attest to the powerful language event storytime offers beginners, perhaps because of the convergence of demonstration, modeling, enlistment, transaction, and sharing (Roser, 1987) in one social time-place.

Storytime also seems to offer teachers a comfort zone for talking with children in new ways about stories, a nonthreatening and pleasure-filled occasion to make fundamental changes in book talk that eventually carries over to the discussions of books that children read for themselves. Storytime is often the place where teachers come to realize the depth and richness of responses that children are capable of making (See Hickman, 1981; Lehr, 1988). In addition, teachers who model some of their own responses as they read aloud (musing, reflecting, associating, comparing, speculating) begin to notice their influence on children's ways of responding—not so much in the mimicking of content but rather in their matching the teacher's diversity in types and levels of thought and talk.

Ms. Gibson read to her kindergartners from *Cloudy with a Chance of Meatballs* (Barrett 1978), a story-in-a-story in which Grandpa tells of the town of Chewandswallow that received its food from the sky:

> And sometimes the wind blew in storms of hamburgers. The people could watch the weather report on television in the morning and they would even hear a prediction for the next day's food (pp. 8–10).

She paused after the passage, stared at the picture, and then mused (almost to herself) "wonder why they'd be interested in that?" That musing produced all sorts of immediate and logical responses from the children, and later in story conversation, further effects of the model showed: "I wonder what if that bread sinks." and "Now wait a minute! How could that be?"

Teachers who offer invitations for the honest reflections of listeners during storytime seem to be rewarded with the children's insights, personal associations, and judgments. Yet, as we observe classroom storytime, we sometimes notice that teachers of young children are more likely to monitor children's comprehension of stories than to invite their thoughts and feelings. Perhaps these teachers are concerned primarily with their responsibility for "teaching" comprehension, or perhaps they are overly familiar with scripted textbook routines. Certainly, children work to make sense of a story—especially when they are young and the story is unfamiliar or complex. Their first expressed responses signal their attention to character identification and plot elements. It is natural that teachers reach to help ensure that children grasp the story line (a part of comprehension) as a way of securing the stage for thinking further. It is only when the opportunity for further thinking is cut short or neglected that a story is treated more as a text to be mastered than a poem to be evoked (Rosenblatt, 1938, 1983; Farrell, 1990).

Far more often, though, we find classrooms in which storytime is a well-established and comfortable routine, important in its own right, but also serving as a benign laboratory in which teachers observe closely the kinds of books and conversational openings that lead to deeper insights and more careful thought about texts. Storytime research has allowed us to understand that even very young children make high level responses, critical judgments, complex inferences, and both personal and literary connections; they recognize themes, discern the craft of the author/illustrator, and delight in doing so. (For a review, see Martinez & Roser, 1991).

And, if all this is within the realm of the child who is not yet reading conventionally, storytime is not so simple anymore. As teachers of beginners prepare for storytime, *they* will be employing more literature study techniques and attending more to literary elements than ever before. They will begin to ask themselves what they need to know and to teach about literature (Eeds & Peterson, 1991). Storytime, still as pleasurable as ever, assumes an instructive role. Even so, its continuing pleasures are ensured by the force of evidence accruing for the influence of storytime on literacy and on children's thought—as reflected in their "talk."

• Guiding Book Talk •

The role of the teacher of literature includes provision of time for children to talk about books. Conversations during storytime shape the conversations children have (even with themselves) about books they eventually read for themselves. Book talk is a critical part of literary response—helping children to "live a little longer in the story experience" (Galda, Cullinan, & Strickland, in press). Dyson (1987) and others (e.g., Cooper, Marquis, & Ayers-Lopez, 1982; Snow, 1983) have argued that when children are engaged in spontaneous talk, when they share experiences, ideas, and opinions, they are engaged in their most intellectually demanding work. Recent work by Eeds and Wells (1989), borrowing from Jim Higgins, aptly characterized the best of book discussions as "grand conversations" in contrast to "gentle inquisitions." Both McGee and Loftus (1991) and Short (1991) underscore the importance of a teacher who participates in discussion rather than dominates it. But what does this participation/nondomination involve? Where do book discussions lead? Where *should* they lead? In a crowded school day, it is appropriate to inquire about the value and direction of book talk.

Why book talk? First, book talk offers chances to think about stories in new ways—to observe, compare, question, and respond and to enjoy new, appreciative relationships with books. Book talk is not merely a "comprehension check," not a list of questions for monitoring readers' grasp of the story line. Rather, book talk is the forum for meaning making. Book talk can begin with "Here's what I'm wondering. . . . " or, "Do you know what this reminds me of?" or, "I wish I could talk to this author because this is what I *really* want to know. . . . " It is a time for finding literary patterns and for exploring themes—for beginning the conversations about stories as events, objects, and messages. All these efforts to express and support ideas through book talk promote the critical thinking of the participants, the thinking that provides the connection among books and between books and the lives of their readers.

Second, book conversations provide a forum for the exchange of ideas. Provision of time for book talk means that teachers value exploration of books and value the interpretations and ideas of readers/listeners. Book talk is the opportunity for readers/listeners to express spontaneously and ever more precisely what they truly want to say about a book—what they notice, what they think, and what they're puzzling over. Ideas are freer and fuller in classrooms in which children are accustomed to discussion, exploration, and exchange. When children present their own ideas in their own ways (perhaps even finding out what they think in the process), they give teachers and others in the group (their conversational partners) the occasion to receive their meanings and to be influenced by them. Responses shared in a group enlighten the responses of others. Through book talk, participants create a literate community (Short & Pierce, 1990) and see through different eyes.

When Sylvia Lopez finished reading her class the big book version of *I Am Eyes: Ni Macho* (Ward, 1978), a beautiful picture book of African flora and fauna, she closed the book to waves of satisfaction around her kindergarten room.

"I love Africa," Lauren said with a sigh.

Sylvia acknowledged the response, "Do you, Lauren?"

Then she asked, "Why?"

"Because Africa copied the zoo!"

Lauren's connection opened the conversation, and "copying" became a conversational focus. For example, this from Felipe: "The artist [Nonny Hogrogian] copied the colors of the pictures into the frames around the pictures."

Planning effective book talk. Many teachers (and researchers) are discovering that good book talk with young children has several definable traits: (1) Good book talk depends upon good books; (2) sometimes it depends upon multiple exposures to those books (rereading); (3) book talk is influenced by a teacher/reader who acknowledges his/her responses; (4) it is dependent upon the physical context for discussion; (5) it is stimulated by a purpose or goal, and (6) it is enriched when books that share characteristics are offered together.

First, good book talk *begins with a good book*—a story worth savoring, turning over in the mind—in short, a book teachers and children want to talk about. Eeds and Wells (1989) noticed that ideas were richer and more insightful in some discussion groups than in others, a finding they traced to teacher and students in combination with a quality story. For young children, too, some books are simply more evocative than others. It makes sense to plan for book talk about those books.

Next, the best book talk often *depends upon more than one reading*. Children's responses to stories change as the book becomes more familiar: They talk more about familiar books; the range of their responses increases, and the focus of talk shifts (Martinez &

Roser, 1985). Familiar books seem to allow children to do more in-depth probing. Some teachers prefer to "preserve a book's integrity" by reading it initially for the story as an event—for the "lived through experience"—and then returning to it for discussion and inspection. But with young children, there is often talk (at some level) during every reading.

When reading in preparation for discussion, effective discussion leaders *keep tabs on their own responses* to the story, making mental or marginal notes as to how they are being affected by the story—what they are thinking about, feeling, wondering about, connecting with, reminded of, and want to share. For example, a teacher planning a discussion of *Stuart Little* (White, 1945, 1973) puzzled over the book's ending and thought about Stuart's inconsistent behavior with his family. She planned to share *some* of her thinking about Stuart's character shifts during book talk. In that way, her own personal responses could fuel the thinking, response, and conversation of the group.

There are still other characteristics of effective book talk: The best book talk *seems to depend upon a conversational setting.* Book talkers who gather face to face in conversation-like groups (rather than aligned in traditional classroom rows) are more likely to have a real discussion, one in which the talk occurs child to child as opposed to child-to-teacher. [For neophyte book talkers, though, there is a natural desire to find audience for one's own thoughts rather than to respond to another's.] As mentioned earlier, many researchers are discovering that teachers who ask fewer questions, participate rather than dominate book discussion, and yet retain a plan for book talk are successful in promoting rich and varied book discussions.

A relatively *simple plan for book talk*—one that can be abandoned or modified as the direction of conversation changes—has been posed by Aidan Chambers (1985) and labelled as "three sharings." Chambers described engaging children in book talk with invitations for the following: (1) the sharing of enthusiasms—talking about what readers observed or noticed and liked; (2) the sharing or puzzlements—talking about what readers wondered about or questioned (*especially* if there are no definitive answers); and (3) the sharing of connections—talking about what connections the text elicits, what the participants are reminded of from other stories or from their own lives.

Chambers's plan for discussion can be combined with Cianciolo/Miller's approach to literature as art, in that the sharing of observations, puzzlements, and connections can occur in response to literature as event, as object, or as message (Fig. 4.1). For example, teachers who initially offer broad invitations for response to the story as *event* can later guide children to consider the story beyond those initial responses and respond to the story as *object* or as *message*. Even very young children can wonder about the artist's technique (puzzlement over text as object) or recall the artist's style in another book (connections associated with text as object). Not intended as a system for categorizing response, this plan offers teachers awareness of how talk can focus and also be extended. Even brief inspection of story talk helps adults realize that children will move beyond recapturing story line and toward issues traditionally associated with the study of literature.

Finally, we have found that *books organized into units* encourage children's book talk and independent reading. Books joined together because they share a theme or topic, because they are reflective of a particular literary form or genre (like legends or folktales), or because they are the works of one author/illustrator help children find relationships across story boundaries. Units help children discover the connections that link literature and better understand that "stories lean on stories" (Yolen, 1977). Good ideas seem to flourish when there are opportunities to explore and connect—to make sense of

FIGURE 4.1

A Plan for Young Children's Story Talk

	Observations	Puzzlements	Connections
EVENT			
OBJECT			
MESSAGE			

[For examples of talk that distributes across these categories, see the Appendix.]

things for one's self and to discover ways of "knowing." Units seem to promote the continuous development of reading, writing, and thinking in response to literature (Roser et al, 1990).

• Beyond Book Talk •

My colleague Jim Hoffman and I have worked with hundreds of teachers and administrators in Texas to devise and offer literature units for classroom use. We have observed these units being taught in over one hundred of these classrooms. Teachers reported that the linked texts increased the children's awareness of the world of books, as well as stimulated divergent responses. Among the evidence of response we have gathered (and are gathering) are classroom Language Charts and teachers' and children's response logs—places in which drawings and writing about books are preserved.

Language Charts. Each set of books that comprised one of our literature units was selected and gathered because of a central focus (e.g., Special Toys, Being Friends, or The Earth Turns 'Round). A guide accompanying each unit suggested instructional goals, response options, and a format for a Language Chart. The Language Chart format was designed to provoke an awareness of the links among stories in a particular unit, and to serve as a record of storytime talk (See Moss, 1984). Physically, the Language Chart was simply a ruled matrix of columns and rows on butcher paper, with column headings labelled with the unit's connecting foci, and with row headings for receiving the title of each book as it was read and talked about. Children's ideas about books—as well as their drawings in response to stories—filled the spaces on the chart, so that the Language Charts colorfully stored the language and creations of negotiated and personal meaning. Following book talk, teachers helped children decide what language should be preserved on the chart; as they wrote, they talked about the idea and the writing itself. Thus, the charts served as a record of talk, as a means of ensuring young children's discoveries about the relatedness of books, and as a place for revisiting and rereading the ideas children offered (See Roser & Hoffman, 1992, for a description of other functions Language Charts served).

FIGURE 4.2

Being Different is Being Special

TITLE	AUTHOR	WHO WAS DIFFERENT?	HOW WERE THEY DIFFERENT?	WHAT MADE THE CHARACTER SPECIAL?
Oliver Button is a Sissy	Tomie de Paola	Oliver	Some kids thought Oliver liked the same things as girls.	Oliver had talent!
Horton Hatches the Egg	Dr. Seuss	Horton	Horton was an elephant but he sat on a nest!	Horton was a faithful friend to sit until the elephant-bird hatched.
William's Doll	Charlotte Zolotow	William	etc.	etc.

Later, we questioned some of our assumptions about Language Charts. We worried that, even though preserving responses on the chart was designed to *follow* rather than guide the book talk, predetermined connections on a Language Chart might focus conversation too rigidly and be resistant to individual discovery. In our newest project in San Antonio, together with a set of unit-experienced teachers, we have moved away from our focused Language Chart formats to more open-ended invitations—patterned after Chambers's work—asking readers what they noticed about the book while they read, what they wondered about or puzzled over, and what connections they had made, linkages between the story and individual lives and between the story and related pieces of literature. The eleven teachers who are experimenting with the revised framework have noticed changes in the ways they themselves think about stories and in the ways they encourage children to respond.

We also questioned whether a group-constructed meaning could occur too rapidly—before there is enough time for independent, personal reflection and response. So, we began to invite children's immediate responses through logs—before the postreading book conversation began.

Response logs. The children we are working with in Northside Independent School District in San Antonio have begun to reflect on a story in response logs immediately after the story is read. They are invited to take a few minutes (three to five) when the book is finished to write what they are thinking or feeling. Kindergarten and first graders write on half sheets of unlined colored paper bound at the top with a plastic comb. The children give their logs such names as "My Own Journal." Logs in the kindergarten are set up like easels when children have finished writing and are ready to talk. After some time for collecting one's own personal thoughts, the journals become a basis for conversation with others.

Ms. Sloan finished reading *Grandfather Twilight* (Berger, 1984), the peacefully quiet story of a bearded gentleman who releases a glowing pearl each evening to end the day in soft twilight. She and her kindergarten children were busily writing in the ways they chose when Ms. Sloan noticed Lucy was covering her paper with dots and sticks. She waited until it was time for book talk for an explanation. Lucy turned her journal toward the class to share, displaying the dots and sticks. "It's a song I wrote about twilight," she said seriously, indicating the "notes." "Can you sing it?"

"Will you show us how?" her teacher asked.

So Lucy sang: "This is the way the dawn begins. This is the way the dusk begins. You must say good-bye to the day." Others solemnly agreed you must indeed say good-bye to the day, because saying hello is only part of a person's responsibility.

"It was poetry," Ms. Sloan told several of us later. "I saw in Lucy's song the influence of our unit (The Earth Turns 'Round) and the important words and ideas of our books and discussions." But Lucy's song may not have found voice if the quiet time for writing had not preceded discussion—if the group had moved too quickly toward a group-constructed meaning. Writing first can preserve the influence of the quietest voices.

Across the hall in Ms. Lopez's room, the children had listened to *Barn Dance* (Martin, Jr., & Archambault, 1986) read aloud:

Right hand! Left hand!

Around you go!

Now back-to back your partner

in a do-si-do.

Seth was busily at work writing in his response log. When he shared, he glanced at his "temporary spelling" and read his idea fluently: "I thought if we could do a barn dance when we are reading the book again because it sounds like a dance." Discussion of the special sounds of dancing words signals the study of literature in kindergarten.

Jeff Davenport shared some of his Meadow Village Elementary first graders' journals from November. After *Rotten Ralph* one child wrote:

> I was sad when Ralph ait the Cooky an poot
> The blloon on the dog and cllnn up the pop coon
> and got sic.

But (as explained below) Mr. Davenport was even more elated with Gabriel's response:

> The Third-Story Cat
> I Love the Part when The Cat Jumped out the windo.
> I Love The Part when The Cat escape and went to
> The Park.

Jeff exulted about Gabriel in writing and gave permission to quote him here:

> "Look, Mr. Davenport! I wrote two stories, " exclaimed Gabriel triumphantly as he held his response journal in my face. To my amazement, Gabriel had written "two stories" about the book we had read that day. This was a great accomplishment for Gabriel. Prior to using response journals my students participated in free writing. For the most part students like Gabriel only drew pictures and very seldom wrote words to accompany these pictures. It was shocking to see "two stories" about *The Third Story Cat* from Gabriel and no picture. In fact since November 4, Gabriel has not drawn a single picture [in his journal] but has responded to each book with words. Not only have Gabriel's writings changed but I have seen an improvement in all of my students' writings. The students enjoy writing about the books

we read each day. Although many of the entries are still evaluative comments, they are personalized by each child's individual reflection on the book. Response journals have been effective in tapping into the thoughts of my students and have been a good way to get their own language down in written form.

Book talk and drawing are powerful tools for organizing thought and for reaching others (Dyson, 1989); still, both Gabriel and his teacher were elated that Gabriel has still another tool for making sense of things coming under his control—writing. Although journals for older students are more broadly researched (e.g., Raphael et. al., 1992; Rogers, 1987; Wollman-Bonilla, 1989), there is still relatively little documentation of young children's responsive journal writing and its influences on book talk and language/literacy growth.

Even so, many of us are seeing for ourselves the influence of writing on discussion. Daphne felt the influence of *Brave Irene* (1986) when she wrote:

Irene showed graet cerij and love in what she had done for her preshis mother. I now that Irene was scard. I was lost in a stor and I had to tell my mom the hole store. I admier her cerij. Irene Irene I like Irene.

When Daphne contributed her insights after collecting these thoughts on paper, her journal entry became a talk "fueler". Many other children responded with talk that began "I had to tell my mom . . . " or "I like her, too, because . . . ."

The teachers we work with write in their journals as the children do and use their journals to support their book talk as the children do. Ms. Gonzales's response log demonstrates her willingness to reach for the center of story, to model through her writing what she drew from the book that connected with her own life, to view qualities of the book, and to puzzle about something that couldn't be immediately answered. She influences her children to be willing to take similar risks. Here is a selection from Ms. Gonzales's response log for *The Flame of Peace: A Tale of the Aztecs* (1987):

> This story made me think of my Mexican heritage and the thought that I am part Aztec also. It made me feel very proud to know that Two Flint had brought peace to the Aztec people; I too believe in peace and justice for all people in the world. This book made me realize again that each person can make a difference in the world to better the lives of others. The Nautl language used throughout makes the book very authentic. I wonder why they began fighting in the first place.

We are learning that personal writing before story talk can enrich the talk, ensure wider participation, and support genuine exchange.

ROLE OF TEACHER AS GUIDE TO LITERACY

If the role of literature infusion is to offer *all* children the best examples of language, to challenge their thinking, and help them to reach for understandings of themselves and others, it serves still another purpose for beginners: it pulls them toward conventional reading. Yesterday in a book store, I overheard two parents talking. The first, describing her out-of-earshot preschooler, said: "He taught himself to read." The other responded, "Don't tell his teacher; it's subversive." The first parent thought that she hadn't had much to do with her young child's learning to read—regardless that she was in a bookstore restocking her supply of children's books. The second thought that teaching to read is a birthright entrusted only to school-teachers and that teachers denounce insurgents when their territory is encroached upon. Neither parent was right.

The lucky bookstore child didn't "teach himself to read," and the teacher will be delighted that he can. His mother defines teaching too narrowly. She made it possible for him to learn to read (and that's teaching) by such "natural practices" as countless hours of talking to him, asking and answering questions, engaging in language and letter play, reading and rereading favorite stories and rhymes, pointing out print when they shopped at the market, providing tools for his writing, modeling reading and writing, and supporting his interest and efforts. But not all children have such literacy backgrounds, and not all children who experience literacy events similar to the bookstore child "teach themselves" so readily. Although the practices of "bookstore" and "library" and "newspaper" parents can't be imported wholesale into classrooms (because classrooms are different from homes), they bear scrutiny because they have taught all of us a great deal about the teaching of literacy.

• Language Play •

Young children learning to talk play with language. They experiment with its sounds ("Han-nah-nah-nah"); they try out its meanings ("You bopperflot!"). In homes in which children are talked to and sung to, bounced rhythmically, and read rhymes, the children come to appreciate the sounds (and satisfactions) of language. They happily supply rhyming words at the end of refrains; they relish the nonsense language of Dr. Seuss. Eventually they come to understand that their language is "segmentable"—that they can take it apart, combine its sounds, and hear the difference in the beginnings of words that rhyme. This set of understandings about spoken language is called phonemic awareness. Not a single ability or insight, phonemic awareness is a predictor of success with conventional reading (Beck & Juel, 1992). Increasingly, there is evidence that home factors such as storytime, word play, and rhymes contribute to this under-standing. Kindergarten and first grade children who participate with predictable books, songs and chants, rhythms and finger plays, word games, "read-alongs" and opportunities to write are learning about the nature of the sounds of their language as they are learning about its meaning and functions. Researchers are also discovering that phonemic knowledge can be supported by learning to read; that is, the more children read, the more they understand about the nature of their language. (Perfetti, Beck, Bell, & Hughes, 1987; Yopp, 1985).

• Shared Reading •

As mentioned earlier, Don Holdaway (1979) transported the practices of home storybook reading to school by enlarging the books to provide visual access to a group, a practice he labelled shared reading. Books selected for enlarged versions (or Big Books) were children's favorites, patterned for their participation and pre-diction, and simple enough so that teachers could make the print bold and visible for a class. Especially when literature in Big Book form has predictable features does it help to propel literacy. Heald-Taylor (1987) described predictable text traits as strong rhythm and rhyme, repeated patterns, refrains, logical sequences, supportive illustrations, and traditional story structures. [Bridge, Winograd, and Haley (1983) reported that children using predictable books learned significantly more target and nontarget words than students using traditional preprimers.]

In shared reading, teachers often read the original versions of the stories first; later, they bring out the enlarged versions. Because Big Books are often homemade, they are not always illus-trated. Illustrations are sometimes left to the children, as one of a variety of book-centered activities available after reading time.

• 95

[When we make Big Books, we tape in children's drawings so that they can be removed and returned to the artist, readying the Big Book for next year's readers.] Typically, children follow along as the teacher reads from the enlarged text, using a pointer to indicate each word. Young readers may predict events or story language. Almost immediately the children chime in, read along, and beg to "read it again." Reading repeatedly ensures familiarity and supports the children's own emergent readings of the stories.

Eventually, Holdaway's experimental program included: (1) discovery—introduction of an enjoyable story with predictable, repetitive structures, opportunities to read along and to problem solve with both story line and written code, experiencing a story that can be returned to on subsequent days; (2) exploration—rereadings, usually on request, for familiarization, enjoyment, deepened understanding and teaching of structures, words, and letter-sounds; (3) independent experience and expression—individual and small group retrieval of the book experience, relying on reading or readinglike behaviors, continued opportunities for enactments, illustrations, and involvement in all the expressive arts.

Big Books are increasingly offered in published form. Through them, teachers help emerging readers work on the development of concepts of print—how books work, how print records and preserves language, how words travel on a page, and the significance of spaces marking them. Big Books, along with children's opportunities to write, support emergent reading and the developing understanding of the written language system.

• Emergent Readings •

Holdaway witnessed, as others have, the great popularity of the original versions of Big Books when they were left in the library corner; he described much trafficking of books between home and school, and also described what he termed "readinglike" behavior—reading that at first may attend solely to pictures or sound like storytelling but may not depend upon the print (See Sulzby, 1985a; Heald-Taylor, 1987, for a description of the behaviors of emerging readers). As children gain competence in shared reading, they eventually follow the print with their eyes, match their voices (and their fingers) with the print, and point out specific words and patterns. In emergent readings, children spend time reading again and again the books that have been read aloud to them; books hold their interest for increasing amounts of time. Observers of young children's literacy learning point to their diligence solving the written language puzzle (Dyson, 1984) as evidence of children at work. The practice children assign themselves (the tenacity with which they peruse familiar books) helps them secure the dependable features of written language and supports their first attempts at reading books that have not been read aloud to them.

• Shared and Independent Writing •

Cindy Sloan puts a morning message on her board every day. Sometimes the message tells the name of a book the class will read that day. Sometimes it's a reminder or an announcement. As she writes, she talks about the letters, letter forms, and words. Children begin their reading/guessing from the rise of the first chalk dust.

"We"

"It starts like We, but it's the name of the day."

"Wednesday."

"Yes, today is Wednesday."

"Wednesday. We . . . "

"Keep going"

". . . can"

(Cindy writes *bring*, but no child responds) "Starts like
  Bryan's name."
"Bring!"
"We can bring . . . "

When the message is completed ("Wednesday. We can bring
our favorite books to the rug."), the children type it. Typing means
they jump up for a capital letter, take one step right as they read
each word, hunker down for a period, clap for an exclamation with
hands above their headS, shimmy for a quotation mark, shrug for a
period, until the whole message is body typed. Cindy says the kids
helped decide the movements for punctuation. Typing the morning
message is just one of the ways they work with written messages
throughout the day.

Shared writing goes on in other ways in kindergarten and
first grade classrooms. Capturing the children's book responses on
Language Charts is one way. Writing at the children's invitation
(as they dictate messages) lets teachers and children talk about
words, letters, and sounds as writing takes shape (Butler &
Turnbill, 1987). Rereading together as the message is being
encoded means children can help decide what should come next
and what conventions are necessary for understanding the message. Shared (or demonstrated) writing is language experience; it
is working together to write a note on the chalkboard to remind
Bart that his mother called to say he should ride the bus; it is composing new-version verses for old favorite songs (Klein, 1989); it is
a king-size thank-you note to the principal for reading to the class;
it is announcements for the hallway, reminders about the open
house, charts with favorite refrains from predictable books, or any
of hundreds of things that really *need* to be written and read that
can be instructive to learners as they are being written.

Writers who see and participate in shared writing take pencil or marker in hand to preserve their own messages—and in the process of moving from drawing to writing, they demonstrate what they are coming to know about literacy (Ferreiro, 1990). From drawing to scribbling to letter strings to the beginnings of syllabic-like spellings, writers draw upon what they are learning from sessions in shared reading and writing, as well as what they learn from one another, as they work out the writing system for themselves—testing their hypotheses with what seems purposeful and functional. A guideline from Sulzby, Teale, and Kamberelis (1989) says it best: "In situations where a teacher would ordinarily invite an older student to write, the teacher should invite a kindergartner or first grader to write as well, being sure to invite them to 'do it your own way' " (p. 70).

• Learning the Code •

Many (but not all) of Holdaway's New Zealand children began to display a remarkable interest and grasp of sounds and alphabet as they engaged in shared reading and writing. Their personal writing shifted toward letterlike strings that they read "with bold assertion" (p. 70). Although there were a few ruffles (one parent wanted his child moved into "a more organized class where he would be taught phonics and not encouraged to think he can read when he can't"), the overall program seemed to be moving children toward conventional literacy, and adjustments were being made as needed. Holdaway initially wondered if children's attention, once claimed by the predictable language of favorite stories, songs, and rhymes, could then be directed to the print. In our experience with Big Books, we have found that once the print is enlarged, the talk about print begins: "Hey, that's in my name," or "I see a lot of m's on that page." The story, already well known and well loved, can offer up its words, spaces, letters, and patterns for scrutiny. The children can already follow the flow of print; they already "talk like a book." Now, teachers and children find, frame, examine, and model their problem-solving processes with print.

In the first half of the twentieth century, the prevailing wisdom was phonics "later"—perhaps after a corpus of sight vocabulary had been achieved. Educators were fearful that too much of the code and its levels of abstraction from meaning would cause children to lose sight of the purpose of reading. With "real" books in the classroom, nothing is really postponed: Good stories are offered from the beginning. When they are reread, emergent readers pay attention to the way written language works. When children, in turn, write their own labels, lists, messages and stories, they begin to test further their understandings about sound-letter patterns. Literature has helped spawn literacy.

A teacher like Phyllis Trachtenburg (1990) preserves story essence as her children read and enjoy a new text for the first time; they return to the story to find patterns of letters and sounds. Children next get to apply a new insight "when reading (and enjoying) *another* whole, high quality literature selection" (p. 649). Trachtenburg calls it a whole-part-whole strategy. Marie Clay (1991) helps children with code by scaffolding the text so that children know the context and direction of the story they will read independently; they then reach for the code in a story they know.

Most teachers of beginners recognize the arbitrary nature of teaching a prescribed sequence of letter-sound associations; one teacher described her dilemma as having created an instructional scheme that caused children to stop asking questions about letters. They seemed fearful that either they hadn't yet "gotten to" that letter or they had forgotten it.

By relying on shared reading as a base for exploring the

code, instruction can be tailored to the print, the class, and the moment: teachers can demonstrate a particular understanding about print at the point of its occurrence in text or follow students' interests in the print or focus on what children are noticing about the nature of written language. Teachers also watch young writers at work, observing what it is that children are struggling with and making sense of in their writing. Shared reading time can then be used to point out some feature of written language that children are exploring on their own. Bobbi Fisher (1991) described how she pointed out the word *is* in a shared reading selection when she noticed that Brad, one of her kindergarten students, continued to struggle with the word in his writing.

AVOIDING THE HAZARDS OF THE TRAIL

With the infusion of literature into classrooms, teachers can model and guide literacy with the same pleasure in books and children that storytime has always permitted. The guidelines are fairly clear: choose good books; let children participate with them actively; help children know them well. Recognize that young children know far more about literacy (in their own ways) than we have ever acknowledged (Sulzby, 1985b) and that they are fonts of information and demonstration about what they know. Classrooms rich in literacy events allow children's "ways of knowing" to emerge and be shaped by literacy models (Huck & Kerstetter, 1987).

Growths in reading and writing develop concurrently and are supportive processes. As with oral language, literacy becomes conventional as approximations of conventional behaviors are struggled with. All beginners need time to "read" and time to "write" in purposeful and meaningful ways. These are the opportunities that make the pieces of the literacy puzzle more manageable. Yet, there always seems to be so little time. Concerns with catching on and catching up put pressures on administrators, teachers, and children. A recent headline in *Education Week* (Viadero, November 5, 1991) announced: "Opposed to Whole Language, Houston Schools Revert to Phonics." The article explained that some teachers and principals felt students from low-income families were doing poorly with the "whole language method" and that the schools would return to traditional phonics-based reading instruction.

Oppositional constructs are the hazards of the trail. Continuing to cast about for an either-or accounting for children's literacy means pitches and rolls in a rough sea. The tools and systems and means of literacy learning are all critical. Children's literacy stems from and depends upon familiarity with literature, a climate of exploration, opportunities to read, think, and write for a variety of reasons, a thinking, writing, responding teacher, and awareness of the written language system. Anything less is too little.

REFERENCES

Adams. M.J. (1990). *Beginning to read: Thinking and learning about print.* Cambridge: The MIT Press.

Babbitt, N. (1990). Protecting children's literature. *Horn Book, 66,* 696–703.

Barrett, J. (1978). *Cloudy with a chance of meatballs.* New York: Atheneum.

Beck, I., & Juel, C. (1992). The role of decoding in learning to read. In S. J. Samuels & A. E. Farstrup (Eds.), *What research has to say about reading instruction* (pp. 101–123). Newark, DE: International Reading Association.

Berger, B. (1984). *Grandfather Twilight.* New York: Philomel.

Brennan, A. D., Bridge, C.A., & Winograd, P. N. (1986). The effects of structural variation on children's recall of basal reader stories. *Reading Research Quarterly, 21,* 91–104.

Bridge, C., Winograd, P., & Haley, D. (1983). Using predictable materials vs. preprimers to teach beginning sight words. *The Reading Teacher, 36,* 884–891.

Butler, A., & Turbill, J. (1987). *Toward a reading-writing classroom.* Portsmouth, NH: Heinemann.

California Department of Education. (1987). *English-language arts framework for California public schools, kindergarten through grade 12.* Sacramento, CA: California State Department of Education.

Carle, E. (1979). *The very hungry caterpillar.* New York: Collins.

Chambers, A. (1985). *Booktalk: Occasional writing on literature and children.* New York: Harper & Row.

Cianciolo, P. J. (1982). Responding to literature as a work of art—An aesthetic literary experience. *Language Arts, 59,* 259–264.

Clay, M. M. (1991). Introducing a new storybook to young readers. *The Reading Teacher, 45,* 264–273.

Cochran-Smith, M. (1983). Reading stories to children: A review-critique. In B. A. Hutson (Ed.), *Advances in reading/language research,* (Vol. 2) (pp. 197–229). Greenwich, CT: JAI Press.

Cochran-Smith, M. (1984). *The making of a reader.* Norwood, NJ: Ablex.

Cooper, C. R., Marquis, A., & Ayers-Lopez, S. (1982). Peer-learning in the classroom. Tracing developmental patterns and consequences of children's spontaneous interactions. In L. C. Wilkinson (Ed.), *Communicating in the classroom* (pp. 69–84). New York: Academic Press.

Cullinan, B. (1987). Inviting readers to literature. In B. E. Cullinan (Ed.), *Children's literature in the reading program.* (pp. 2–14). Newark, DE: International Reading Association.

Cullinan, B. (1989). Latching on to literature: Literature initiatives take hold. *School Library Journal, 35*, 27–31.

de Paola, T. (1978). *Clown of God.* San Diego: Harcourt, Brace Jovanovich.

de Paola, T. (1979). *Oliver Button is a sissy.* San Diego: Harcourt Brace Jovanovich.

Durkin, D. (1966). *Children who read early: Two longitudinal studies.* Columbia University: Teachers College Press.

Dyson, A. H. (1984). Reading, writing, and language: Young children solving the written language puzzle. In. J. M. Jensen (Ed.), *Composing and comprehending* (pp. 167–176). Urbana, IL: National Council of Teachers of English.

Dyson, A. H. (1987). The value of "time off task": Young children's spontaneous talk and deliberate text. *Harvard Educational Review, 57*, 396–420.

Dyson, A. H. (1989). *Multiple worlds of child writers: Friends learning to write.* Columbia University: Teachers College Press.

Eeds, M., & Peterson, R. (1991). Teacher as curator: Learning to talk about literature. *The Reading Teacher, 45*, 118–126.

Eeds, M., & Wells, D. (1989). Grand conversations: An exploration of meaning construction in literature study groups. *Research in the Teaching of English, 23*, 4–29.

Farrell, E. J. (1990). Introduction: Fifty years of literature as exploration. In E. J. Farrell & J. Squire (Eds.), *Transactions with literature: A fifty-year perspective* (pp. ix–xiii). Urbana, IL: National Council of Teachers of English.

Feitelson, D., Kita, B., & Goldstein, Z. (1986). Effects of listening to stories on first graders' comprehension and use of language. *Research in the Teaching of English, 20*, 339–356.

Ferreiro, E. (1990). Literacy development: Psychogenesis. In Y.M. Goodman (Ed.), *How children construct literacy: Piagetian perspectives.* Newark, DE: International Reading Association.

Fisher, B. (1991). *Joyful learning: A whole language kindergarten* (pp. 12–25). Portsmouth, NH: Heinemann.

Galda, L., Cullinan, B., & Strickland, D. (in press) *Language and the child.* San Diego: Harcourt Brace Jovanovich.

Goodman, K., Shannon, P., Freeman, Y., & Murphy, S. (1988). *Report card on basal readers.* Katonah, NY: Richard C. Owen.

Green, J. L., & Harker, J. O. (1982). Reading to children: A communicative process. In J. A. Langer & M. T. Smith-Burke (Eds.), *Reader meets author/bridging the gap: A psycholinguistic and sociolinguistic perspective* (pp. 196–221). Newark, DE: International Reading Association.

Heald-Taylor, G. (1987). Predictable literature selections and activities for language arts instruction. *The Reading Teacher, 41*, 6–12.

Hickman, J. (1981). A new perspective on response to literature: Research in an elementary school setting. *Research in the Teaching of English, 15*, 343–354.

Hickman, J. (1983). Classrooms that help children like books. In N. Roser & M. Frith (Eds.) *Children's choices: Teaching with books children like* (pp. 1–11). Newark, DE: International Reading Association.

Hoffman, J.V., Roser, N. L., & Farest, C. (1988). Literature sharing strategies in classrooms serving students from economically disadvantaged and language different home environments. In. J. E. Readence & R. S. Baldwin (Eds.), *Dialogues in Reading Research* (pp. 331–338). Chicago: National Reading Conference.

Hoffman, J., Roser, N., Battle, J., Farest, C., & Isaacs, M.E. (1990). Teachers' developing insights about the use of children's literature for language and literacy growth. In J. Zutell & S. McCormick (Eds.), *Literacy theory and research: Analyses from multiple paradigms* (pp. 89–98). Chicago, IL: National Reading Conference.

Hoffman, J., Roser, N., Battle, J., Farest, C., Myers., P., & Labbo, L. (1991). Evaluating the effects of a read-aloud/response program. In J. Zutell & S. McCormick (Eds.), *Learner factors/teacher factors: Issues in literacy research and instruction* (pp. 297–303). Chicago, IL: National Reading Conference.

Holdaway, D. (1979). *The foundations of literacy.* New York: Ashton Scholastic.

Holdaway, D. (1982). Shared book experience: Teaching reading using favorite books. *Theory into Practice, 21,* 293–300.

Huck, C. S., & Kerstetter, K. J. (1987). Developing readers. In B. E. Cullinan (Ed.), *Children's literature in the reading program* (pp. 30–40). Newark DE: International Reading Association.

Hunt, L. C. (1969). Con-challenger of the basal reading program. In N. B. Smith (Ed.) *Current issues in reading.* Newark, DE: International Reading Association.

Jensen, J., & Roser, N. (1987). Basal readers in the language arts program. *Elementary School Journal, 87,* 375–383.

Klein, A. M. (1989). Meaningful reading and writing in a first-grade classroom. *Elementary School Journal, 90,* 185–192.

Lattimore, D. N. (1987). *The flame of peace: A tale of the Aztecs.* New York: Harper Collins.

Lehr, S. (1988). The child's developing sense of theme as a response to literature. *Reading Research Quarterly, 23,* 337–357.

Lehr, S. (1990). *The child's developing sense of theme: Responses to literature.* Columbia University: Teachers College Press.

McCormick, S. (1977). Should you read aloud to your children? *Language Arts, 54,* 139–143, 163.

McGee, L.M., & Loftus, F. (1991, December). *An exploration of meaning construction in first graders' grand conversations.* Paper presented at the National Reading Conference, Palm Springs, CA.

Martin, Jr., B., & Archambault, J. (1986). *Barn dance.* New York: Henry Holt.

Martin, Jr., B., & Archambault, J. (1989). *Chicka chicka boom boom.* New York: Simon & Schuster.

Martinez, M., & Roser, N. (1982). Literature in the reading program: Tracing roots. *Reading Professor, 8,* 23–30.

Martinez, M., & Roser, N., (1985). Read it again: The value of repeated reading during storytime. *The Reading Teacher, 38,* 782–786.

Martinez, M., & Roser, N. (1991). Responding to literature in the elementary grades. In J. Squire, J. Jensen, J. Flood, & D. Lapp (Eds.), *Handbook of research on teaching the English language arts* (pp. 643–654). New York: Macmillan.

Martinez, M. G., & Teale, W. H. (1989). Classroom storybook reading: The creation of texts and learning opportunities. *Theory into Practice, 28,* 126–135.

Mason, J.M., Peterman, C. L., & Kerr, B. M. (1989). Reading to kindergarten children. In D. S. Strickland & L. M. Morrow (Eds.), *Emerging literacy: Young children learn to read and write.* Newark: DE: International Reading Association.

Moir, H., & Curtis, W. (1968). Basals and bluebirds. *Elementary English, 45,* 623–626.

Morrow, L. M. (1984). Reading stories to young children: Effects of story structure and traditional questioning strategies on comprehension. *Journal of Reading Behavior, 16,* 273–288.

Morrow, L. M. (1988). Young children's responses to one-to-one story readings in school settings. *Reading Research Quarterly, 21,* 330–346.

Morrow, L. M., O'Connor, E. M., & Smith, J. K. (1990). Effects of a story reading program on the literacy development of at-risk kindergarten children. *Journal of Reading Behavior, 22,* 255–276.

Moss, J. F. (1984). *Focus units in literature: A handbook for elementary school teachers.* Urbana, IL: National Council of Teachers of English.

Naylor, P. R. (1991). *Shiloh.* New York: Atheneum.

Newton, E. S. (1967). The basal primer may be deceptively easy. In W. K. Durr (Ed.), *Reading instruction: Dimension and issues* (pp. 244–246). New York: Houghton Mifflin.

Perfetti, C. A., Beck, I., Bell, L. C., & Hughes, C. (1987). Phonemic knowledge and learning to read are reciprocal: A longitudinal study of first grade children. *Merrill-Palmer Quarterly, 33,* 283–319.

Raphael, T. E., McMahon, S. I., Goatley, V. J., Bentley, J. L., Boyd, F. B., Pardo, L. S., & Woodman, D. A. (1992). Research directions: Literature and discussion in the reading program. *Language Arts, 69,* 54–61.

Rogers, T. (1987). Exploring a sociocognitive perspective on the interpretive process of junior high school students. *English Quarterly, 20,* 218–229.

Rosenblatt, L. M. (1938; 1983). *Literature as exploration.* (4th ed.). New York: The Modern Language Association of America.

Roser, N. (1987). Relinking literature and literacy. *Language Arts, 64,* 90–97.

Roser, N. L., & Martinez, M. (1985). Roles adults play in preschoolers' response to literature. *Language Arts, 62,* 485–490.

Roser, N.L., Hoffman, J.V., & Farest, C. (1990). Language, literature, and at-risk children. *The Reading Teacher, 43,* 554–559.

Roser, N.L., & Hoffman, J.V. (1992). Language charts: A record of story time talk. *Language Arts, 69,* 44–52.

Russavage, P.M., Lorton, L. L., & Millham, R. L. (1985). Making responsible instructional decisions about reading: What teachers think and do about basals. *The Reading Teacher, 39,* 314–317.

Shannon, P. (1987). Commercial reading materials, a technological ideology, and the deskilling of teachers. *Elementary School Journal, 87,* 307–329.

Shaw, C. G. (1947). *It looked like spilt milk.* New York: Harper & Row.

Short, K.G. (1991). *Talking about literature.* Paper presented at the national Reading Conference, Palm Springs, CA.

Short, K. G., & Pierce, K. M. (1990). *Talking about books.* Portsmouth, NH: Heinemann.

Silvey, A. (1990). Editorial: Visual literacy. *The Horn Book, 66,* 132.

Smith, N.B. (1986). *American reading instruction.* Newark, DE: International Reading Association.

Snow, C. E. (1983). Literacy and language: Relationships during the pre-school years. *Harvard Educational Review, 53,* 165–189.

Steig, W. (1986). *Brave Irene.* New York: Farrar, Strauss, & Giroux.

Sulzby, E. (1985a). Children's emergent reading of favorite storybooks: A developmental study. *Reading Research Quarterly, 20,* 458–481.

Sulzby, E. (1985b). Kindergarteners as writers and readers. In M. Farr (Ed.), *Advances in writing research, volume one: Children's early writing development* (127–199). Norwood, NJ: Ablex.

Sulzby, E., Teale, W. H., & Kamberelis, G. (1989). Emergent writing in the classroom: Home and school connections. In D. S. Strickland & L. M. Morrow (Eds.), *Emerging literacy: Young children learn to read and write* (pp. 63–79). Newark, DE: International Reading Association.

Teale, W. H. (1984). Reading to children: Its significance for literacy development. In H. Goelman, A. A. Oberg, & F. Smith (Eds.), *Awakening to literacy* (pp. 110–121). London: Heinemann.

Teale, W. H., Martinez, M. G., & Glass, W. L. (1989). Describing classroom storybook reading. In D. Bloome (Ed.), *Classrooms and literacy* (pp. 158–188). Norwood, NJ: Ablex.

Trachtenburg, P. (1990). Using children's literature to enhance phonics instruction. *The Reading Teacher, 43,* 648–654.

Tunnell, M. O., & Jacobs, J. S. (1989). Using "real" books: Research findings on literature based reading instruction. *The Reading Teacher, 42,* 470–477.

Venezky, R. (1987). A history of the American reading textbook. *Elementary School Journal, 87,* 247–265.

Viadero, D. (1991, November 20). Opposed to whole language, Houston schools revert to phonics. *Education Week.*

Waber, B. (1972). *Ira sleeps over.* Boston: Houghton Mifflin.

Ward, L. (1978). *I am eyes: Ni macho.* New York: Scholastic.

White, E. B. (1945, 1973). *Stuart Little.* New York: Harper & Row.

Wells, G. (1986). *The meaning makers: Children learning language and using language to learn.* Portsmouth, NH: Heinemann.

Wollman-Bonilla, J. E. (1989). Reading journals: Invitations to participate in literature. *The Reading Teacher, 43,* 112–120.

Yolen, J. (1977). How basic is SHAZAM? *Language Arts, 54,* 545–651.

Yopp, H. K. (1985). Phonemic segmentation ability: A prerequisite for phonics and sight word achievement in beginning reading? In J. A. Niles & R. V. Lalik (Eds.), *Issues in literacy: A research perspective* (pp. 330–336). Rochester, NY: National Reading Conference.

CHAPTER 5

...

MULTICULTURAL LITERATURE: ISSUES IN TEACHING AND LEARNING

Violet Harris
University of Illinois

CHILDREN'S LITERATURE ACHIEVED A LEVEL of unprecedented prominence in the 1980s. McDowell (1988) labelled children's book publishing as one of the fastest-growing segments of publishing and one of the most profitable. Even now, for some bookstores, children's books represent one-fourth to one-third of book sales. Evidence of the prominence of children's literature can be found not only in sales figures but in the lines of teachers and children at "meet the author" sessions and made-for-television movies based on children's literature, such as *Sarah, Plain and Tall* (MacLachlan, 1985). Some of the most notable evidence of the importance of children's literature is the expansion of literature-based instruction, the inclusion of extended literature excerpts in basal readers, the existence of new children's literature journals, and the proliferation of children's literature conferences. All of these developments bode well for the present and future of children's literature.

Amid the contentment and justifiable congratulatory comments are voices of concern. The concerns focus on a variety of issues that suggest the importance of children's literature in literacy instruction today. Goodman (1988) identified one area of concern, which he labelled the "basalization" of children's literature. By this term, Goodman meant the alterations of original text in order to control vocabulary level and difficulty, changes in content, the reduction of text, and the changes in syntax for lowered reading levels. Goodman argued that these and other changes resulted in the loss of original style and wit and less natural language (p. 31). The examples he cited also suggested a lack of integrity on the part of publishers who approved changes that changed the very nature of some works. Goodman questioned why publishers included children's literature in basals only to destroy the literature.

Author Natalie Babbitt (1989) identified another crucial concern. Children's books in hardback range in cost from $10.95 to $21.95, and paperbacks range in price from $2.95 to $7.95. These are not insignificant amounts for school districts that desire to adopt a literature-based approach to reading instruction or parents who wish to purchase literature for their children. It is possible to pay less for books through various book club specials such as those offered by Trumpet, Lucky, or See Saw. But, as Babbitt warned, the costs of children's books might well make book ownership among some children an indicator of higher class or something that is determined by higher class status. Babbitt expressed concern for those children who cannot afford to purchase lavishly illustrated picture books or expensive hardbacks. *More, More, More Said the Baby* (Williams, 1990) and *The Way Things Work* (1988) are but two examples of Babbitt's concern.

Nancy Larrick (1991) celebrated the new prominence of children's literature and its role in literacy instruction in the phrase, "Give Us Books! Give Us Wings!." She also lamented the appearance of a new trend in publishing: teachers' guides designed to accompany tradebooks. Larrick argued that these new guides were modeled along the lines of basal readers and criticized their cost, length, and inclusion of extensive, detailed exercises that destroyed literary pleasure. She also criticized the myriad uses teachers put children's literature to, which had little to do with enjoyment of literature, such as teaching children's phonics or mathematical operations.

One consistent concern expressed by Rudine Sims Bishop (1990; 1991) is the need to provide all children with literature that reflects the cultural experiences and traditions of people of color. "In my view, a people's story includes their literature as well as their history, and that becomes part of the argument for having multicultural literature available in schools and libraries" (p. ix). A number of authors chronicle the day-to-day activities, cultural celebrations, and perspectives of African, Asian, Latino, and Native Americans. Yet many teachers are unaware of this literature's existence or do not perceive of its relevance for Euro-American students. Advocates of multiethnic and multicultural literature attempt to fill this void, especially since notions of multiculturalism have assumed greater urgency in schooling.

Multiculturalism has assumed increasing importance for a number of reasons. Many view it as an appropriate mechanism for imbuing children with notions of racial and ethnic tolerance as well as a method for initiating fundamental changes in schooling. Children's literature has escaped some of the internecine canon wars evident at the secondary and college levels. At these levels, analyses based on race, class, and gender elicit two extreme reactions, with neutral and moderate voices ignored in the clamor. Opening up the canon for diversity is an issue that will remain prominent in discussions about literary curricula for a considerable period of time.

In this chapter I will examine some of the potential problems that may emerge when educators attempt to implement a multicultural literary curriculum at the elementary level. The discussion is organized in the following manner: (1) examination of conceptions of multiculturalism; (2) identification of theoretical and philosophical underpinnings; (3) analysis of the goals of multiculturalism; (4) opposition to multiculturalism; (5) issues in teacher training; and (6) student concerns.

CONCEPTIONS OF MULTICULTURALISM

It has become quite fashionable when discussing education to note the increasing ethnic and racial diversity of schools, particularly urban schools. A number of statements written about diversity and schooling have almost become clichés (Gay, 1975; 1983; 1988; Sleeter & Grant, 1985; Gollnick & Chinn, 1986; Banks, 1975; 1981; 1983; 1991). The statements incorporate many of the following ideas:

1. Most urban schools will become the exclusive domain of the poor or underclass, who are African American or Latino;

2. Approximately 5 percent of the teaching force will consist of African American teachers by the year 2000;

3. Students of color need teachers who are like them so that they may have role models;

4. Students of color and girls will have improved self-esteem and motivation to succeed in school if the curriculum includes information about the achievements of people of color and women;

5. African American and Latino students should emulate Asian American students who are generally hard-working, ambitious, motivated to learn, and who perform well in science and math;

6. White students will become the minority in many urban school systems, and some teachers will have no choice but to teach in schools in which the students are nonwhite. Therefore, teachers should prepare to work with non-white students;

7. White students need some information about people of color because they are projected to comprise a significant portion of the work force and improved relations would result from increased knowledge and understanding.

These and similar statements surface in popular and scholarly journals, in the electronic media, and at education conferences. A number of conferences have been planned to discuss the best solutions for ensuring that insurmountable problems do not arise. Inherent in these statements and discussions is the assumption that schools can implement fundamental social changes that other societal institutions either cannot or are unwilling to implement. The questions arise as to what multiculturalism is, what fostered its emergence, and how it has manifested itself in children's literature.

A number of labels are synonymous with multicultural diversity, or multiculturalism (Banks, 1983; Sleeter & Grant, 1985). Among the current parallel terms are pluralism, cultural pluralism, cultural diversity, and multiethnic diversity. Other labels or metaphors exist as well, such as patchwork quilt, salad bowl, tapestry, or mosaic. These terms imply differences that manage to combine to form a variegated yet harmonious whole. Multiculturalism, depending upon which conception one supports, focuses on issues of race/ethnicity, gender, class, language differences, "ableism," and religion (Sleeter & Grant, 1985). Some proponents have expanded the category to incorporate anti-racism, heterosexualism, environmentalism, "thinism" (the perpetuation of the body ideal represented by fashion models), and peace/pacifism (Ellsworth, 1989). Despite the current tendency among some to include any component of difference under the rubric "multicultural," most academics interested in multiculturalism emphasize race, class, gender, handicap, and, to a lesser extent, language variation. Sleeter & Grant (1985) define *multicultural education* as the term educators use to describe "educational policies and practices that recognize and affirm human differences and similarities related to gender, race, handicap, and class" (p. 137). At the center of the various conceptions of multiculturalism are beliefs that the United States is comprised of various cultures whose members contribute in similar and unique ways to the development of a national culture and that equality for all should emerge as a prevailing national theme.

A number of factors served as catalysts for the emergence of multicultural education. These include the modern civil rights movement, the women's movement, attempts to implement bilingual education, and the struggles over curriculum content designed to ensure that the contributions of excluded groups, especially people of color and women, are included. These struggles for social change affect all societal institutions, including schools. Many view schools as the ideal place to implement these societal changes.

Multiculturalism has manifested—and continues to manifest—itself in various ways in children's literature. First is the struggle to make available literature that depicts people of color in authentic, nonstereotyped fashion. African Americans were in the vanguard of this effort. For instance, as early as 1910 scholar W. E. B. Du Bois wrote of the need for literature that would not stereotype or denigrate African American children.

> "I sought to encourage the graphic arts not only by magazine covers with Negro themes and faces, but as often as I could afford, I portrayed the faces and features of colored folk. One cannot realize today how rare that was in 1910. The colored papers carried few or no illustrations; the white papers none. In many great periodicals, it was the standing rule that no Negro portrait was to appear and that rule still holds in some American periodicals." (Du Bois, 1971, p. 271).

Du Bois attempted to provide authentic literature through the publication of *The Brownies' Book* (1920–21), a children's magazine, and through collected biographies such as *Unsung Heroes* (Ross, 1920). In addition, African Americans continuously advocated the creation of authentic literature throughout the twentieth century; for example, librarians Charlemae Rollins and Augusta Baker and authors Arna Bontemps and Langston Hughes worked to fulfill this dream (Harris, 1990). An article published by Nancy Larrick in the 1960s brought up the issue of ethnic diversity in children's literature. The article, "The All-White World of Children's Books," (1965) created a stir among publishers, librarians, parents, and teachers. Larrick documented that of the 5,200 children's books published between 1962 and 1964, only 6.7 percent included a reference about or illustration of an African American child. Larrick's finding generated concern because the United States was in the midst of the civil rights movement and in the middle stages of the Cold War. How could politicians and others use the United States as a model of democracy for the rest of the world when African Americans were discriminated against and excluded from textbooks? A new world order necessitated the expansion of democratic principles to all. Publishers responded in a number of ways. They hired increasing numbers of African Americans in all phases of book production. They sponsored contests to identify promising African American authors. Most important, they published the works of these newly identified authors.

By the end of the 1960s, an increase in the number of books about African Americans was apparent. The portrayal of others, Latinos, Asians, and Native Americans lagged considerably, and unauthentic portraits were prevalent. Their portrayals would improve in a marked manner by the mid-1970s. The 1970s marked an improvement in the number of books about people of color, girls and women, and the disabled. However, publishers and the public did not institutionalize many of the advances and gains of the 1960s and '70s. Downward trend was apparent in the 1980s, so much so that the number of books about people of color declined to less than 5 percent (Norton, 1990; Bishop, 1990). Today, the major issues still center on the availability of multicultural literature, its marginalization in children's literature canons, and issues of authenticity.

Flagrant stereotypes of the type associated with *The Story of Little Black Sambo* (Bannerman, 1899; 1923) or *The Five Chinese Brothers* (Bishop & Wiese, 1938) rarely appear. However, some subtle stereotypes and, occasionally, blatant stereotypes appear. For example, many Native Americans are dismayed with the portrayal of the "Indian" in *The Indian in the Cupboard* (Moore & MacCann, 1988). The author depicted the Indian as a savage who was violent and uncivilized. Similarly, some criticized *Jake and Honeybunch Go to Heaven* (Zemach, 1982) for its stereotyped depiction of African American religious traditions. The criticisms directed against these and other books stem from more than righteous indignation. The criticisms are rooted in sociological and psychological theory and philosophy. For example, some argue that stereotyped depictions promote racist ideology, cause Euro-American children to have unsupported notions of superiority, create feelings of inferiority among those who are stereotyped, and deny children the right to develop authentic perceptions of people unlike themselves (Larrick, 1965; Bishop, 1990).

THEORETICAL AND PHILOSOPHICAL UNDERPINNINGS

The theoretical and philosophical origins of the various conceptions of multiculturalism are multiple and somewhat nebulous. For example, Sleeter and Grant (1988) argue that more has been written about multicultural theory as it relates to gender than to race and ethnicity or any of the other categories. They suggest that educators usually adopt supporting theories from anthropology and sociology. According to Sleeter and Grant, the theories generally selected are theories of cultural pluralism and cultural transmission. Within cultural pluralism, four theories dominate: assimilation, amalgamation, classical cultural pluralism, and modified cultural pluralism.

Assimilation theory posits that contact with a majority culture will result in members of a minority culture acquiring the values, mores, lifestyles, and beliefs of the majority or dominating culture. *Amalgamation* suggests that a new cultural form emerges when varying cultures interact. In *classic cultural pluralism*, distinct cultural entities maintain their individual identities. *Modified cultural pluralism* suggests that some groups will assimilate and also maintain distinct cultural attributes to varying degrees while other groups will retain unique cultural attributes.

Sims (1982) developed a critical taxonomy to describe contemporary African American children's literature that parallels the aforementioned theories. Critics from other groups have adapted and modified Sims's work to examine their literature as well. Sims delineated three categories: social conscience, melting pot, and culturally conscious books. *Social conscience books* attempted to promote harmonious relations by emphasizing the similarities among cultures rather than differences. The central purpose of these books was to provide Euro-American children with an appropriate model of interaction. Four types of stories appeared in this category: stories about school desegregation, stories about integration, stories about African Americans who fight against discrimination with assistance from Euro-American friends, and stories about African American children who learn to "get along with whites." *Melting pot books* closely parallel the goals of assimilation. These books were written in such a manner that they present the notion of a homogeneous American culture with no racial conflicts. Three types of stories appear in this category: stories from the perspective of white children, stories about interracial friendships, and stories about middle-class African Americans. The last category, *culturally conscious books*, captures features of classic cultural pluralism and modified cultural pluralism. Culturally conscious books represent an authentic body of literature written about and for African American children. These stories focus on the African and Southern heritages of African Americans, fighting racism and discrimination, everyday experiences, urban living, friendships, family, and stories about growing up.

Sleeter and Grant (1988) expanded concepts of multiculturalism to include ideology. Ideology would incorporate systems of beliefs, values, and actions that are supported through various institutions. Ideology is explained through theories of cultural transmission, social learning, and modelling. They identified three implications of these theories that relate to multiculturalism: (1) "[that] children learn through a complex variety of messages" (2) "[that] not everyone in society shares identical knowledge and beliefs"; and (3) the notion of "cultural compatibility" (pp. 150–152). Specifically, a variety of individuals, institutions, and cultural artifacts shape children's knowledge; individuals do not have equal access to cultural knowledge, and ways of thinking, interacting, and communicating are not the same in each culture. What these ideas suggest is that no one model of multiculturalism will serve the needs of all individuals in the variety of cultural contexts in which they exist.

All of this suggests that individuals should make explicit the philosophical, theoretical, and ideological underpinnings of their multicultural literature curricula. Doing so forces the individual to recognize the complexities of the many issues related to developing and implementing multicultural literature curricula. Foremost among these issues is determining the purposes for developing such curricula and the goals to be obtained from them.

GOALS OF MULTICULTURALISM

In an ideal society unfettered by the realities of inequity, stratification, or intergroup hostilities, the literature of each group categorized under the rubric "*multicultural*" would automatically appear in literary canons. Under such circumstances, the only reason for including the literature would be to provide some aesthetic pleasure, entertain, or inform or to address human concerns in a universal way. Reality does not reflect this ideal.

A number of goals are expected to result from the implementation of a multicultural curriculum. Gollnick and Chinn (1986) identified six goals of multicultural education. These were for students to "learn basic academic skills; acquire a knowledge of the historical and social realities of U. S. society in order to understand racism, sexism, and poverty; overcome fear of differences that leads to cultural mis-understandings and intercultural conflicts; function effectively in their own and other cultural situations; value cultural differences among people and to view differences in an egalitarian mode rather than in an inferior-superior mode; and understand the multicultural nation and interdependent world in which they live" (pp. 255–256).

Sleeter and Grant (1988) conceived of the goals of multicul-tural education (one which is also social reconstructionist) as those that affect society in a global manner and those that affect individuals at the school level. They identified the societal goals as to foster equal opportunity in schools and to support structural equality, pluralism, and the diversity in lifestyles. In a similar fashion, Banks (1991) delin-eated seven goals for a multicultural curriculum. Among these goals were: (1) develop decision making and social action skills; (2) help stu-dents analyze events from diverse perspectives; (3) develop cross-cul-tural competency; (4) provide cultural and ethnic alternatives; (5) reduce ethnic encapsulation (help students eliminate parochial senti-ments); (6) expand conceptions of what it means to be human; and (7) help students master essential reading, writing, and computational skills. These goals share in common the desire to promote tolerance, increase knowledge, and reform or reconstruct society in order to establish greater equality and equity.

When one wants to implement a multicultural literature cur-riculum, these goals and others related to literature must be consid-ered. A multicultural literature curriculum would introduce students to a range of literature, created by a variety of individuals, that pro-vides aesthetic enjoyment, promotes tolerance for diversity, improves understanding of human relations, develops critical consciousness, and encourages students to effect some type of social change. It would seem that "whole language," or emancipatory literacy, curric-ula would fulfill these objectives. Several tenets of whole language support multiculturalism. First, the emphasis on using authentic texts parallels the advocacy of authentic depictions and texts in multiculturalism. Second, proponents of whole language encourage the use of materials that will interest and motivate children; this, too, follows tenents of multiculturalism that suggest diversity in materials will foster self-esteem and motivate students. Most important, the emphasis on empowerment in whole language is comparable to its espousal in multiculturalism. One may well inquire whether these expectations are appropriate ones to place on literature. Do authors intend for their works to change individuals and societies? Or do authors simply find literature a convenient outlet for their creativity?

Historically, children's literature has never existed simply to provide pleasure (Kelly, 1985). Adults appropriated children's literature for a variety of extraliterary purposes, including socialization. This overt didacticism and inculcation continues today; one need only read the Berenstain Bears series in order to validate this observation. The advocacy of literature to advance a multicultural literature curriculum is well within tradition. The manner in which the goals of a multicultural literature curriculum are realized depends, in part, on the particular approach to multicultural education adopted. Banks (1991) identified four ways of implementing the multicultural curriculum. The contributions approach "focuses on heroes, holidays, and discrete cultural elements" (p. 26). In the additive approach "content, concepts, themes, and perspectives are added to the curriculum without changing its structure" (p. 26). In the transformation approach, "the structure of the curriculum is changed to enable students to view concepts, issues, events, and themes from the perspective of diverse ethnic and cultural groups" (p. 26). The last method, the social action approach, involves "students make[ing] decisions on important social issues and take[ing] actions to help solve them" (p.26). Banks argued that each approach has problems and that effective responses to ethnic realities would occur when the curriculum was transformed and students acquired decision-making and social action skills (p. 29).

One can easily implement the various approaches in a multi-cultural literature curricula. For example, one can implement the contributions approach by simply adding books that focus on heroes, holidays, or discrete cultural elements such as biographies of famous individuals (McKissack's [1990] biography of Jesse Jackson or Say's [1990] picture book about an Asian American who becomes a bull-fighter, or books about holidays, Kwanzaa, Cinco de Mayo, Hanukkah, or Chinese New Year or discrete cultural elements such as Yarbrough's [1979] book on cornrow hairstyles. Similarly, a teacher can create a multicultural curriculum that incorporates the transfor-mation approach by identifying a topic or theme and examining it from the perspectives of various groups. For instance, growing up or coming of age stories can be examined in every culture. The additive approach can be accommodated by simply expanding reading lists and including multicultural works on the list. Finally, the social action approach can be used by having students read literature that prompts introspection and discussion, and that inspires students to believe or act in certain ways. Think about powerful works, for example, *Roll of Thunder, Hear My Cry* (Taylor, 1976) or *The Journey* (Hamanaka, 1989) that present poignant accounts of the struggles of African and Japanese Americans. Few students should be able to read these works and still harbor racist or bigoted thoughts.

Sleeter and Grant (1988) identified five approaches to multi-cultural education comparable to those identified by Banks. The first approach emphasizes "teaching the exceptional and the culturally different" with the major goal being to prepare students to fit into mainstream society. The purposes of the second approach, improv-ing human relations, are to "promote positive feelings among stu-dents and reduce stereotyping, thus promoting unity and tolerance in a society composed of different people" (p. 75). The single-group studies approach is "characterized by attention to a single group." The fourth approach, multicultural education, focuses on "education policies and practices that recognize, accept, and affirm human differences and similarities related to gender, race, handicap, and class. The final approach, education that is multicultural and social reconstructionist, "means that the entire education program is redesigned to reflect the concerns of diverse cultural groups" (p. 175).

At the very least, the adoption of a multicultural literature curriculum should result in students and teachers acquiring more knowledge. Ultimately, a fully realized curriculum would result in significant changes in a number of institutions and in the lives of teachers and students. A number of people advocate these instrumental uses of literature (Taxel, 1991). However, opposition to some facets of multiculturalism exists.

Opposition to Multiculturalism

The opposition to multiculturalism, though not directed at fundamental goals, centers primarily on some of the unintended consequences or those perceived as unintended. Broudy (1975), for instance, critiqued the new cultural pluralism. He argued that the more "extreme and militant" forms of cultural pluralism promoted the treatment of minority cultures as separate and equal, that some cultures did not share a traditional ideal of a common culture, and that some groups would not participate in the "culture of the country" and in the "cultural and artistic achievements of the human race" (pp. 174–175). Broudy's arguments reflect an understanding of the need for expanded curricula that reflect the contributions of heretofore omitted groups, but he held to an assimilationist view as the ultimate goal.

Ravitch (1990) offered a critique of "particularistic pluralism" that mirrored Broudy's argument. According to Ravitch, particularistic pluralism encouraged collective guilt, a sense of rage and victimization, and did not promote reconciliation among various groups. She advocated a type of pluralism that promoted shared sets of political and moral values and a sense of nationhood. Ravitch questioned whether a multicultural curriculum would result in improved academic achievement and enhanced self-esteem of individuals categorized under the rubric "multicultural."

A different kind of criticism of multiculturalism was evident in the work of McCarthy (1988). He offered a critique of multicultural education as a temporary stopgap whose intent was the reduction of the effects of racism, sexism, and class bias. But the crucial problem with multicultural education was the lack of recognition for the belief that equality and equity in education would require total, possibly radical, reorganization of schooling. Other critiques appeared in the popular press: *Newsweek* (December 24, 1990) and *The New York Times* (December 8, 1990). In these articles, opinions were divided on the efficacy of including analyses based on race, class, gender, and multiculturalism. These ideological stances were characterized by some as the "new McCarthyism," the tyranny of the New Left, or the politically correct. Many believe that expansion of curricula would result in a "balkanization of knowledge," lead to the demise of educational excellence, or the promotion of mediocrity.

For the most part, opposition to multiculturalism in children's literature is not vocal or evident in the popular press or the academic press. Partly this is due to the marginalized status of children's literature as evidenced by the term "kiddie lit." Most of the opposition to children's literature centers on the depiction of families, the perceived promotion of "anti-family" values, or the promotion of satanism or alternative lifestyles. Opposition to multicultural literature will probably manifest itself in terms of an attitude that the books are not for white children, in the steering away of children from books because they are not perceived to relate to children's lives, or in opposition to content. Some type of teacher training is needed to help teachers acquire the knowledge and skills needed in order to help them feel comfortable sharing multicultural literature.

TEACHER TRAINING

Awareness of the need for teachers receiving some training in multicultural education became an official policy of at least one accreditation agency. The National Council for the Accreditation of Teacher Education revised its accreditation standards in 1979 and mandated that teacher training programs include a multicultural education component. This mandate has not resulted in substantial change. Two scenarios suggest possible teacher responses to mandates.

The state of Illinois mandated that schools provide a unit of instruction on African American history, women's history, and the Holocaust. The law did not specify what constituted a unit or how much time teachers would have to allocate to each unit. The director of secondary curriculum for a school system in Illinois lamented the types of responses she received from teachers. Many of the teachers felt insulted that their perspectives were not solicited. Others resented adding new elements of study to what they perceived of as an overloaded curriculum. A few openly admitted that they resented having to teach these subjects. Still others felt unqualified to teach the new requirements.

Consider another scenario in the same town. A university professor, who teaches a reading methods course, invites another professor to the class to lecture on multicultural literature. The professor provides the students with two articles she has written on African American children's literature in order to provide students with essential background information before the lecture. Prior to the lecture, the professor prepares a bibliography of professional references and trade books and gathers a variety of multiethnic literature reflecting a range of genre, themes, and interest levels. The professor reads excerpts to the students and discusses several issues related to multicultural literature. She also provides opportunities for students to peruse the books and ask questions. The professor notes that the students share the books with each other and write down titles not listed on the bibliography. Undoubtedly, many of these students will integrate multicultural literature in their curricula.

The two scenarios provide a glimpse of some of the problems with mandates and the positive responses that *can* result when teacher educators combine their talents and expertise to encourage preservice teachers to include multiethnic literature in their literacy programs. One problem involves teacher empowerment; another, decisions about curricula content, and still another, teacher knowledge. What would constitute teacher empowerment within the realm of multicultural literature curricula?

Ideally, teachers would work with administrators and to some extent, with parents and students to fashion a program advancing the goals of multiculturalism. They would determine objectives, approaches, content, and evaluation criteria. Decision making would not reside with administrators; the various entities would share power. Some teachers, parents, and students, those with a greater amount of expertise or interest, would assume roles as leaders, guides, or mentors. The discussions, more than likely, would prove lively as complete agreement could not be expected and compromise would figure prominently in decisions. Along with teacher empowerment would come calls for increased accountability, especially when multicultural literature curricula are mandated by states or school boards. Teachers would then have to assume some of the responsibility for the successes and failures of multicultural curricula.

Decisions about content, more than likely, would mimic the "canon wars" waged in adult literature (for example, A. Matthews's essay on the Modern Language Association Conference, *The New York Times Magazine*, February 10, 1991, pp. 42–43, 57–59, 69).

Opponents of multiculturalism argue that many advocates wish to remove traditional classics and replace them with mediocre works or that the expansion of the curriculum would result in children not having opportunities to acquire a shared literary heritage comprised of the best in literature. Literary canons, by their very nature, are exclusionary and subject to the judgments, whims, and tastes of those with definitive aesthetic and ideological stances. Literary canons are not neutral entities. Further, few advocates of multiculturalism call for the wholesale removal of classics from reading lists. Instead, they argue that other works, which can be multicultural in content, meet and occasionally exceed standards of literary excellence (although such standards seldom result from consensus) and deserve inclusion in literary canons because they provide aesthetic enjoyment and offer insight on the human condition through the prism of a particular culture.

Other issues regarding content are likely to emerge as well. For instance, many works of multiethnic literature contain vernacular language. *All Us Come Cross the Water* (Clifton, 1973) is an example. Some teachers are quite uncomfortable with vernacular language. They do not feel comfortable pronouncing the words or believe that the literature encourages the use of nonstandard forms. Author Clifton noted the objections of well-meaning and well-intentioned adults who would limit children's access to this and other works because of the language. Clifton (1981) responded to critics thus:

> This leads me to talk about the question I get asked more often than any other, "Why do the children in your books talk like that? Why do you write that dialogue?" I've written nineteen children's books and I sometimes wonder which dialogue they're talking about. They're not talking about Everett Anderson, who talks in rhymed iambic pentameter, which not many people do today. They're not talking about that; that's unauthentic talk. Everybody doesn't talk the same way and everybody doesn't talk the same way all the time. And people notice this. If you are teachers and you are talking to each other informally you talk

differently from the way you talk to students. Now if you don't admit that, that is your problem . . . I have a book called *All Us Come Cross the Water.* I know about "of," I know about "across." But the little boy in that book does not say, "All of us came across the water." If you are asking me to write that, you are asking me to be unauthentic as an artist, and I'm simply not going for it (pp. 34–35).

Another problematic issue is exemplified over the controversy involving textual authenticity. Who is best qualified to write about a culture, a member of the culture or someone who is not a part of the culture? Which portrayal is more authentic? Sims (1984) addressed the issue directly when she questioned why author Belinda Hurmence chose to write about African American culture in *A Girl Called Boy* (Hurmence, 1982). Sims argued that Hurmence was well within her rights to depict any culture. The central issue for Sims was why an author would write about a culture with which she lacked familiarity. Perhaps the issue is best exemplified in the furors that developed over books such as *The Indian in the Cupboard* (Banks, 1980), and *The Slave Dancer* (Fox, 1973). The authors or illustrators of these books were accused of perpetuating stereotypes.

Still another issue relates to the graphic depiction of violence, poverty, drugs, race relations, sex, and family relations in some of the books. Author Walter Dean Myers (January, 1991, Ohio State Children's Literature Conference) addressed some of these issues. He stated that he received criticism from adults who thought his portrayal of Harlem's crack problem or the Vietnam war were not suitable for children. In response, he stated that he understood objections to the books but felt a need to portray the lives of some of the children he encountered.

A related issue concerns the interpretation of historical events and periods. Many teachers have had traditional interpretations of historical events such as the treatment accorded Native

Americans, usually ensconced in discussions about Manifest Destiny or the westward expansion. What happens when those teachers read Dee Brown's *Bury My Heart At Wounded Knee* (1974), which details the atrocities of the westward expansion? Will teachers dismiss this insider perspective or internalize the recounting to an extent whereby they do not share the information with students? A range of responses is possible.

The issue of teacher knowledge about multiculturalism looms large. Many teachers simply do not possess any knowledge about multicultural literature. Further, they do not know where to seek that information. It is folly to mandate required courses when teachers cannot provide information. It is highly unlikely that significant numbers of teacher educators possess knowledge about multicultural literature given the fact that many states do not require a general children's literature course for certification. Clearly a need exists for more systematic training of teachers, not simply the provision of booklists, but a type of training that results in the institutionalization of multicultural ideals. A number of resources exist, but many teachers will probably acquire their knowledge in an independent fashion. For example, they will have to attend children's literature conferences, subscribe to children's literature journals, and maintain contact with organizations such as the Association for the Study of Afro-American Life and History and the Children's Interracial Books Council that evaluate literature and publish curriculum guides. Finally, teacher training will have to focus on students.

STUDENT CONCERNS

Proponents of multicultural curricula unabashedly state their goal of imbuing students with a sense of tolerance for diversity, improved intercultural relations, increased knowledge about the traditions and histories of various cultures, and the need for social change, along with instruction in basic competencies (Gay, 1983).

Further, they argue that the goals of multicultural curricula apply to all students. Yet, according to Grant and Sleeter (1985), most teachers do not include a multicultural component in their curricula. On those occasions when teachers incorporate multiculturalism, it appears in those schools with a significant population of students of color. An erroneous assumption underlies this policy—the belief that Euro-American students neither need nor want multicultural education.

Students are an integral component of multicultural education, and proponents contend that some teachers will have to eliminate biases toward students of certain ethnicities, races, or classes (Gay, 1983; Gollnick & Chinn, 1986). They also suggest that teachers will need to develop strategies that accommodate individual differences. Students' attitudes deserve attention as well. Not every student wants to acquire a multicultural perspective. What recourse does a student have when the goals of multiculturalism conflict with values of the student's family? For example, a teacher shares the collection of creation myths entitled *In the Beginning* (Hamilton, 1988). Some students or their parents object to the book on the basis that it conflicts with their religious beliefs. Does the teacher excuse the students from discussions, attempt to alter their views, or encourage them to view the selections on the basis on literary criteria alone or as an example of a particular genre? Many would argue that there are some rights of individuals that should not be diminished for what is perceived as the greater good. Similarly, the goal of social change may not rest with students who may or may not possess the critical consciousness or maturity needed to effect social change.

Other issues, such as school climate and the accommodation of students' learning styles, affect students as well. The school, teachers, and administrators must value multiculturalism and actively seek to incorporate it in all or most aspects of schooling. When students perceive that adults value multicultural literature and multiculturalism, it is likely that they, too, will develop tolerant attitudes or at least begin to perceive the need to do so. Overt actions, such as book and pictorial displays, the presence of teachers who are members of the groups identified as multicultural, and the inclusion of the groups' achievements in texts, help create an environment that values diversity.

The issue of students' learning styles is a controversial one. Some argue that children of color display verbal interaction patterns, interpersonal interaction patterns, and ways of thinking in direct contrast to those expected by teachers (Gay, 1988). Those who advance this argument do not contend that these are inherent differences in intellectual abilities, but rather they argue that cultural and ethnic patterns can differ from the "white, middle class" model many teachers expect. However, one should approach this argument with caution because of the potential abuse it can elicit. For instance, carried a step further, a teacher could argue that African American children cannot enroll in physics courses or write sonnets because the cultural interaction patterns, traditions, or ways of thinking and learning do not promote the acquisition of such knowledge. Legitimate cultural differences exist, but these are not applicable to every member of a particular group; nor should these differences be held responsible for the failure rates of many students of color. Nonetheless, these and other issues will have to be investigated as schools become more diverse.

The preceding discussion highlights some of the factors that will arise when teachers, parents, students, and others demand curricula reflecting the diversity of the country. These demands, if fulfilled, should result in fundamental reconceptualizations of schooling, knowledge, and the goals of schooling.

REFERENCES

Babbitt, N. (1989). Protecting children's literature. *The Horn Book Magazine, 66,* 696–703.

Banks, J. (1975). The implications of ethnicity for curriculum reform. *Educational Leadership, 32,* 168–172.

Banks, J. (1981). *Multiethnic education. Theory and practice.* Boston: Allyn and Bacon, Inc.

Banks, J. (1983). Multiethnic education at the crossroads. *Phi Delta Kappan, 65,* 559–563.

Banks, J. (1990). *Teaching strategies for ethnic studies.* (5th ed.). Boston: Allyn and Bacon, Inc.

Bishop, R. S. (1990). Window, mirrors, and sliding glass doors. *Perspectives, 6,* ix–xi.

Bishop, R. S. (1991). African American literature for children: Anchor, compass, and sail. *Perspectives, 7,* ix–xii.

Broudy, H. (1975). Culturalism: New wine in old bottles. *Educational Leadership, 32,* 173–175.

Clifton, L. (1981). Writing for Black children. *The Advocate, 1,* 32–37.

Du Bois, W. E. B. (1971). *Dusk of dawn.* New York: Schocken Books.

Ellsworth, E. (1989). Why doesn't this feel empowering? Working through the repressive myths of critical pedagogy. *Harvard Educational Review, 59,* 297–324.

Gay, G. (1975). Organizing and designing culturally pluralistic curriculum. *Educational Leadership, 32,* 176–183.

Gay, G. (1983). Multiethnic education: Historical developments and future prospects. *Phi Delta Kappan, 65,* 560–563.

Gay, G. (1988). Designing relevant curricula for diverse learners. *Education and Urban Society, 20,* 327–340.

Gollnick, D., & Chinn, P. (1986). *Multicultural education in a pluralistic society* (2nd ed.). Columbus, OH: Merrill.

Goodman, K. (1988). Look what they've done to Judy Blume!: The basalization of children's literature. *The New Advocate, 1,* 29–41.

Grant, C. A. (1975). A carrot in a pot of water is not vegetable soup: Racism in school and society. *Educational Leadership, 32,* 184–188.

Grant, C. A. (1983). Multiethnic education and the quest for equality. *Phi Delta Kappan, 65,* 582–585.

Grant, C. A., Boyle, M., & Sleeter, C. (1980). *The public school and the challenge of ethnic pluralism.* New York: The Pilgrim Press.

Harris, V. J. (1990). African American children's literature: The first one hundred years. *Journal of Negro Education, 59,* 540–555.

Kelly, R. G. (1985). Literary and cultural values in the evaluation of books for children, *The Advocate, 4,* 84–100.

Larrick, N. (1965). The all-white world of children's books. *Saturday Review, 48,* 63–65, 84–85.

Larrick, N. (1991). Give us books! . . . but also . . . give us wings! *The New Advocate, 4,* 77–83.

McCarthy, C. (1988). Rethinking liberal and radical perspectives on racial inequality in schooling: Making the case for nonsynchrony. *Harvard Educational Review, 58,* 265–279.

McDowell, L. (1988, April 18). Profitable renaissance for children's books. *The New York Times, 48,* 63–65, 84–85.

Moore, O., & McCann, K. (1988). The ignoble savage: Amerind images in the mainstream mind. *Children's Literature Association Quarterly, 13,* 26–30.

Ravitch, D. (1990). Diversity and democracy. *American Educator, 14,* 16–20. 46–48.

Sims, R. (1982). *Shadow and substance.* Urbana, IL: Nationa Council of Teachers of English.

Sims, R. (1984). A question of perspective. *The Advocate, 3,* 145–155.

Taxel, J. (1991). Notes from the editor: On the politics of children's literature. *The New Advocate, 4,* vii–xii.

Children's Books

Bannerman, H. (1899; 1923). *The story of Little Black Sambo.* New York: Harper & Row.

Banks, L. (1980). *The Indian in the cupboard.* New York: Doubleday.

Bishop, C., & Wiese, K. (1938). *The five Chinese brothers.* New York: Coward–McCann.

Brown, D. (1974). *Bury my heart at Wounded Knee.* New York: Holt, Rinehart & Winston.

Clifton, L. (1973). *All us come cross the water.* New York: Holt, Rinehart, & Winston.

Fox, P. (1973). *The slave dancer.* New York: Bradbury Press.

Hamanaka, S. (1989). *The journey.* New York: Franklin Watts.

Hamilton, V. (1988). *In the beginning.* New York: Harcourt Brace Jovanovich.

Hurmence, B. (1982). *A girl called Boy.* New York: Houghton Mifflin.

McCauley, D. (1988). *The way things work.* Boston: Houghton Mifflin.

McKissack, P. (1990). *Jesse Jackson.* New York: Scholastic.

McLauchlan, P. (1985). *Sarah, plain and tall.* New York: Harper & Row.

Ross, E. (1920). *Unsung heroes.* New York: Du Bois & Dill Publishing Comp.

Say, A. (1990). *El Chino.* New York.

Taylor, M. (1976). *Roll of thunder, hear my cry.* New York: Bantam.

Williams, V. (1990). *More, more, more said the baby.* New York: Greenwillow.

Yarbrough, C. (1979). *Cornrows.* New York: Coward, McCann and Geoghegan.

Zemach, M. (1982). *Jake and Honeybunch go to heaven.* New York: Farrar, Strauss, and Giroux.

CHAPTER 6

ABILITY GROUPING AND THE TEACHING OF LITERATURE

James Marshall
University of Iowa

A BUILT-IN FEATURE OF AMERICAN SCHOOLING seems to be ability tracking, also called streaming or grouping (Mitchell & Haycock, 1988; Oakes, 1985; Goodlad, 1984). Initiated in response to the large influx of immigrant children and the demands of an industrial economy at the turn of the century (Mitchell & Haycock, 1988), tracking now often guides instruction in the language arts from prereading through advanced-placement literature. Though the research on the effects of tracking is widespread, one major finding seems clear: tracking leads to significant differences in the daily learning experiences of students (Oakes, 1985). Students in different tracks, in other words, are not usually provided uniform access to knowledge and skills in the classroom, and these differences in access lead, over time, to increased differences in performance (Goodlad, 1984).

This chapter will explore how ability tracking helps shape literature instruction in secondary classrooms. Drawing on both national surveys and a series of case studies of English classrooms, I will explore how the differences among ability tracks lead to differences in the curriculum, in the goals of teachers, in the attitudes of students, and finally, in the language of instruction itself.

THE CURRICULUM

We begin by examining the titles of books that students in upper-ability and lower-ability classes are asked to read in school. Applebee's (1989) national survey of schools found that the ten most frequently assigned book-length works in the two groups were those presented in Figure 6.1.

FIGURE 6.1

Most Popular Titles by Track

UPPER TRACK		LOWER TRACK	
Romeo and Juliet	44%	Of Mice and Men	25%
Macbeth	44%	The Outsiders	23%
Huck Finn	38%	The Pearl	21%
To Kill a Mockingbird	35%	Romeo and Juliet	17%
Julius Caesar	34%	Macbeth	17%
Hamlet	34%	The Pigman	14%
The Scarlet Letter	34%	To Kill a Mockingbird	13%
The Great Gatsby	31%	Julius Caesar	13%
Lord of the Flies	28%	Call of the Wild	13%
The Crucible	28%	The Diary of a Young Girl	12%

Perhaps the most obvious difference between the groups is that students in the upper-ability classes are more frequently asked to read classic, canonical literature. Four of the texts listed for the upper-ability students are Shakespearian plays and three are established American classics (*Huck Finn, The Scarlet Letter,* and *The Great Gatsby*). In contrast, only three Shakespearian plays are frequently assigned to lower-ability classes (*Hamlet* disappears from the top ten), and while the novels of Steinbeck and London are perennial favorites, they do not have the same canonical status as those by Twain, Hawthorne, and Fitzgerald.

And there are further contrasts. The upper-ability list, for instance, includes only one work written by a woman (Harper Lee's *To Kill a Mockingbird*), while the lower-ability list includes three (*Mockingbird*, Hinton's *The Outsiders*, and Anne Frank's *The Diary of a Young Girl*). The upper-ability list contains only four works written in the twentieth century (*To Kill A Mockingbird*, *The Great Gatsby*, *Lord of the Flies*, and *The Crucible*), while the lower-ability list contains seven (everything, in fact, except the plays by Shakespeare). Finally, there is a significant difference in the relative length of individual works on the two lists. *Of Mice and Men*, *The Outsiders*, *The Pearl*, and *The Pigman* can properly be considered novellas. *Call of the Wild* and *The Diary of a Young Girl* are quite short. And even *Macbeth* is Shakespeare's shortest play. The upper-ability list, meanwhile, contains no works that are especially short.

Even an elementary analysis such as this suggests that students in the two ability groups are receiving very different kinds of literature instruction. For better or worse, students in the upper-ability tracks are more frequently exposed to classic works in the traditional canon, while students in the lower-tracks read shorter, more contemporary works. Such an arrangement means that lower-track students may not be getting instruction in that literature usually associated with cultural literacy and college admission, while the upper-ability students may be getting few opportunities to read and discuss literature that is more directly relevant to their own lives. Simply in terms of what they are asked to read, then, students in the two groups may be missing a part of what makes literature instruction an important feature of secondary education.

But there is another kind of information in Figure 6.1 that also suggests the profound curricular differences between upper-ability and lower-ability literature classes. In the upper-ability group, there seems to be a relatively broad consensus of what books ought to be taught. *Romeo and Juliet* is taught in 44 percent of the schools surveyed, *The Scarlet Letter* in 34 percent, and *Lord of the Flies* in 28 percent. While clearly there is room for choice among the surveyed schools, there is also a kind of agreement about what it is important for upper-ability students to read and discuss.

But agreement about the curriculum for lower-ability students seems much less clear. In fact, there is less consensus about the most frequently taught book in lower-ability classrooms (25 percent for *Of Mice and Men*) than there is for the book ranked tenth in frequency for the upper-ability classrooms (28 percent for *The Crucible*). Not only, then, are students in lower-ability classrooms reading different works from their upper-ability peers, they are also more likely to be reading different works from other students in lower-ability classrooms nationwide. The absence of a strong consensus about what students in lower-ability classes ought to read suggests that there may be a greater effort with these students to individualize instruction and to tailor the selection of texts to students' own interests. But it might also suggest that students in these classes are often presented with a make-do curriculum consisting of short and available texts rather than a thoroughly reasoned curriculum grounded in theory and established practice. Whatever the case, it seems obvious that students will come to read, discuss, and write about different kinds of literature depending on the ability track in which they are placed.

They will not only approach different texts in their classes, however; they will also approach those texts in different ways. Applebee's (1989) study of exemplary English programs suggests the different instructional strategies employed in upper-track and lower-track literature classrooms. Figure 6.2 provides the relevant information.

FIGURE 6.2		

Primary Emphases during Instruction

	UPPER TRACK	LOWER TRACK
Close Textual Analysis	59%	52%
Student Response	42%	33%
Thematic	36%	27%
Social History	20%	11%
Moral Values	7%	13%
Literary History	11%	4%
Intellectual History	7%	0%

Note: Percents total more than 100 because some classes had more than one primary emphasis.

What is most salient about these percentages, of course, is that teachers and students in lower-track classrooms apparently do less of almost everything than students in upper-track classes—less textual analysis; fewer calls for student response; insignificant emphases on social history, literary history, or intellectual history. In fact, the only emphasis that is greater in lower-track than in upper-track classrooms is on moral values—a finding that may say more about teachers' attitudes than about students' interests. Clearly, students in the lower-track classrooms are doing fewer of the kinds of things we usually associate with the study of literature in school. They are receiving less practice in the analysis of texts and in the articulation of their own response than their peers in upper-track classrooms. And when combined with the differences in the kinds of texts students are asked to read, these differences in approach suggest how powerfully the curriculum in literature is changed as we move across ability tracks. We will look now at how teachers working at the different ability tracks articulate their goals and their strategies in teaching literature.

TEACHERS

Sarah is a teacher working with twelfth-grade advanced-placement English students. In an interview with us, she described some of the tensions she felt working with such a group.

> When I first started teaching, I probably lectured twice a week and I'd feel dizzy at the end of the day from talking so long and hard and practically standing on my head as I saw them fade. It really is true: you work way too hard doing that. And I worked awfully hard as I fed every question to them. You don't have to do that for very long before you realize that you can only formulate so many manipulative questions in order to get them to say what you think they ought to say—what you want them to say—before you have to realize that you just have to admit to the kids, "see, I was trying to get you to say something and you didn't say it. . . . " So I'm trying to relinquish my control as a teacher. I'm trying to turn it over. But with my college-bound kids I feel strongly that somebody else is dictating to me what I should do with the literature. And I think it's too easy to say, "Well, the heck with that. We'll just do what we want to do." I don't want to shortchange my kids. They are going to have certain demands made of them—expectations. I want them to be prepared for that. I don't want to think that I did them wrong just because I have another set of ideas about what should be done with literature.

There are at least two oppositions at work in Sarah's thinking about her teaching, both involving the issue of control. On the one hand, she contrasts the teaching she did fresh out of college

("I'd probably lecture twice a week . . . ") with the teaching she is attempting now ("So I'm trying to relinquish my control as a teacher. I'm trying to turn it over"). On the other hand, she contrasts that commitment to relinquishing control in her teaching with pressures to prepare her students for the demands that will be made of them ("[W]ith my college-bound kids, I feel strongly that somebody else is dictating to me what I should do with the literature"). In other words, Sarah wants to give up the control that seemed so unproductive in the early years of her teaching ("I saw them fade"), but she feels she cannot because she herself is not in control of the curriculum ("I want them to be prepared"). Whatever is keeping Sarah from teaching the way she would like to teach is located outside of her classroom: it is a set of standards or expectations about college-bound students that she cannot resist without taking the risk that she will "shortchange" her kids.

The teachers working with middle-track students also described tensions in their work. But here the conflicts seemed to have a different source. Doug Overstreet, for instance, working with a group of eleventh-grade middle-track students, had these observations about his own teaching.

> The class is discussion-based. The students do the talking about the literature. (But) the problem I've noticed is that I'm doing a lot more talking than I wish I had to . I wish that I could do less and let the students do more. And there are a variety of reasons for that. Some unavoidable things such as the fact that the class is large and that it's the first in the morning. But that's kind of like putting the blame somewhere else. "Well, it's the first-period class, they don't talk, it's not my fault, they're still sleeping or something like that." But I don't think that's the main reason. Part of it lies in myself. I know for

example, this book, *The Great Gatsby*, I'm trying to decide how much I need to teach from the book. Do I need to point out every little detail? I feel compelled to do so. I seem to be pointing things out to them all the time. And maybe what I'm waiting idealistically is for some student to say, "Mr. Overstreet, did you see that line on page 127? What a great line! I think that he was trying to say . . . " and so on. And instead, I'm leading them to conclusions that I have already formulated, I think. I think that might be what I'm doing rather than allowing them to formulate their own conclusions.

Doug seems to be describing some of the same kinds of tensions that Sarah articulated. Like her, he is concerned that he may be too much in control (I'm leading them to conclusions that I've already formulated") instead of allowing them the freedom to find their own way into the text ("I wish I could do less and let the students do more"). But what seems most telling about Doug's observations is that the problem is not, as it was with Sarah, pressure from outside the classroom to prepare students for college; the problem, Doug decides, is rather with himself—with the established patterns of his own teaching. In some ways, he may be more free than Sarah in deciding on an instructional approach, but that freedom cannot be exercised until Doug can imagine alternatives to the approach in which he himself has been schooled. The issue, as with Sarah, remains one of control, but the source of the difficulty has shifted from outside to inside the classroom, from those who tell teachers what to teach to the teacher himself.

The source of difficulty shifts once again when we listen to teachers working with lower-track students. Jean Taggert, for example, works with twelfth-grade students in an inner-city school in New York.

It's such a battle. You have absolutely no idea. The anger. The resistance. They have never been asked to read before out of the room. And that is the truth. They can't believe that I am expecting them to read this story by themselves. The stories that I know are tough, I start it and set up the characters. I get names on the board so they're not confused, and the setting, where it takes place. And I move as far as them reading aloud. I read some myself, asking some to read who are willing to do that, who are good readers. We establish what I consider security information so that people are not so intimidated. But they read the two opening paragraphs and they are lost. They are not readers and they are tired. And they are annoyed that they are being asked to read at all.

As with Sarah and Doug, we can quickly locate the issue of control as central to Jean's reflections on her teaching. She provides a good deal of instructional support for her students—putting the characters' names on the board, making sure students understand the setting, reading the story out loud. She gives the students what she calls "security" information—basic knowledge that will enable them, she hopes, to make moves into inference and interpretation. But as she makes very clear, these moves are seldom made because the students themselves are discouraged and uninterested in the task she has set. They are angry, Taggert reports, and resistant, and finally tired. Like Sarah and Doug, Jean wants students to participate more fully in the activities she designs. But like them, she continues to do most of the talking—not, like Sarah, because of pressures from outside the classroom, and not, like Doug, because of internalized patterns of teaching. Jean continues to do most of the talking because the students themselves have given up. It is to the perspectives of those students that we will now turn.

STUDENTS

Perhaps the most obvious effect of tracking on students is in their attitude toward themselves and toward their peers. At least some of them seem to have internalized the hierarchical instructional arrangements in their schools and used them to map the social territory they inhabit. Rich, for example, was a ninth-grade, upper-track student in California who told us the following:

> At Aragon High School you have the cream of the crop on one hand and the bottom of the barrel on the other. And that's good because you get a good look at all phases of life. Only in athletics, though, do you get a good mix of people. In classes, there's English for the advanced, English intermediate, and English low—you know, the dummies.

What seems most striking about Rich's observations here is not just his naively revealing use of metaphor ("cream of the crop" and "bottom of the barrel"), but the way he sees the distribution of talent in his school as in itself educational ("that's good because you get a good look at all phases of life"). For Rich, school is not just a place where he studies and meets his friends, but a microcosm of those "phases of life" that he must come to understand as part of growing up. There is little question of where Rich sees himself positioned among those phases. With a kind of wink, he refers to the "dummies" who do not share his and, he assumes, our perspective.

But what is the perspective of those who do not, like Rich, see themselves among the "advanced." Perhaps not surprisingly, they too read the tracking system as a kind of metaphor for larger social arrangements. Don, for instance, was a twelfth-grade student in a middle-track classroom. He said:

I think at a young age, we were separated into the smart people, the regular, and the dumb. And the smart people, everybody knew, were above everyone else and they were expected to work and they were going to learn. The middle kids said, "Ah, forget it. We don't care. We'll get through high school." And the dumb kids, they still get help and they are pushed and eventually could probably become smarter than the middle-track people. The middle-track people are not interested and they don't want to continue on, whereas I think the lower-track kids do want to learn but they don't understand. The top track kids do want to learn and they do understand.

As a basic, deterministic analysis of tracking in schools, it might be difficult to do better than this. According to Don, there seem to be at least two elements necessary to success in school—intelligence and effort. The "smart people" have both ("they were expected to work and they were going to learn"). The middle kids lack the will to learn ("Ah, forget it. We don't care. . . . "), while the "dumb" kids have the will (they "do want to learn") but not the intelligence ("they don't understand"). Effort seems to be as important as intelligence since Don feels that the lower-track students may eventually become "smarter than the middle-track people." Still, these moves have already been determined by decisions made long ago ("[A]t a young age we were separated"), and thus what Don and his peers do in school—the effort they show, the help they receive—has in a sense been scripted by the tracking system itself.

When we listen to students in the lower-tracks—the "dummies," in Rich's terms, the "dumb kids" in Don's—the same kind of determinism seems to prevail. Here, however, it is not just the tracking system but the economic system that gives rise to the distinctions with which students must deal. David was a twelfth-grader in an inner-city school in New York who put it this way:

Like we got sides in this school, the scumbags and the higher people. People look at you just cause you got a leather jacket or you got your head shaved and you got long hair, got Doc Marten boots or holes in your pants, people look at you like you're scumbags. You ain't got no polo shirt on, you know? Gold around your neck, driving a BMW to school. You're garbage. We have a totally different life, the way we live. We just don't have a life where we wake up in the morning, go to school, do our school work, and then go home, do our homework, and then we go to bed or eat dinner with our Mommy and Daddy, you know? We don't have a life like that.

Like Rich, David sees the lines that separate students from one another as reflective of larger social divisions. What makes his observations so striking, however, is that such divisions look very different when viewed from his perspective rather than from Rich's. The tracking system, for David, is simply one more invidious distinction with which he must deal. The precision and intelligence of his analysis belie his label as "lower-track," while his passion and anger reveal the human cost of that label.

There are other costs as well. If tracking helps shape the curriculum, the attitudes of teachers, and the attitudes of students, then we would expect it to alter the nature of the instruction as well. We will turn now to a discussion of classroom episodes within the various ability tracks.

THE LANGUAGE OF INSTRUCTION

How do classroom discussions unfold in upper-track, middle-track, and lower-track classrooms? In some ways, we would expect similarity: after all, the subject is the same, the teachers have been comparably educated, and the conventions governing classroom discourse are firmly in place in all three contexts. On the other hand, though, the differences in texts and attitude that we have already examined would lead to noticeable differences. Let us begin by looking at one perhaps typical episode from an upper-track classroom. The students are college-bound eleventh and twelfth graders, and the text is Jerzy Kosinski's *Being There*.

> TEACHER: Now, I just want to take one additional look before I make the transition here to the institutions that Kosinski deals with. I often put emphasis on beginnings and endings, the first paragraph of a short story, the beginning, the first line of a poem. I'm a Poe-ist in that regard, Edgar Allan Poe's theory about the significance of every word, every line in a short story. The significance of a first line, that it should not be wasted. You don't have that kind of time. And here, rather than just toss this off, not only does the first paragraph often serve to give some kind of focus, but then we end up with another literary technique here. When writers start throwing similes and metaphors at you, boom! Indication! Alert time! You know, he's taking the time to make some form of comparison, either direct or indirect, whatever the case may be. What's he doing in paragraph one?
>
> STUDENT: Comparing people to plants.
>
> TEACHER: Comparing people to plants. OK. Using what technique?
>
> STUDENT: Simile.
>
> TEACHER: Simile. OK. There's that key word *like* in there. OK, in that regard, plants are like people. Are there more, perhaps some ways in which plants are not like people?
>
> STUDENT: They don't have feelings.
>
> TEACHER: No feelings. Interesting simile, but to what extent does the simile actually apply?

Perhaps the most obvious observation we can make here is how clearly the teacher controls the discussion. The teacher speaks more frequently than any individual student, and the floor is returned to him after each student's turn. More important, perhaps, his turns are significantly longer than his students' turns. Students offer only a sentence, sometimes only a single word in their turns, while the teacher repeats and then elaborates upon what students have said, adding detail and raising related questions.

But just as clear as the teacher's control of the discussion is his focus on literary form. He is interested in showing his students the importance of textual beginnings, and he does this by indicating the source of that interest ("I'm a Poe-ist in that regard") and by leading them through a close reading of Kosinski's first paragraph ("What's he doing in paragraph one?"). He gives, at least in this episode, little attention to the plot, characters, or setting of the novel—he is more interested in how it works as a piece of art and in abstracting from this one case a more general principle of literary criticism ("When writers start throwing similes and metaphors at you, boom! Alert time!"). He seems to be inviting his students to examine the text as a critic might, to savor its technical sophistication, and to become more knowledgeable connoisseurs of how such art is put together. Nowhere in this episode (or elsewhere), though, does he try to connect the text to student's practical concerns or personal histories.

We can see how these concerns can shift with ability track by examining an episode from a middle-track classroom. Here the students are tenth graders, and the text is John Hersey's *Hiroshima*.

TEACHER: "Now did you get any names for Father Kinesorge's people?"
STUDENT: "Cieslik."
TEACHER: "Spell it to me."
STUDENT: "C-i-e-s-l-i-k."

Teacher:	"OK, Cieslik. I think Cieslik is going to come out bad. He's going to end up with all kinds of glass in his back. Do you know anything about getting a piece of glass in your skin?"
STUDENT:	"It stays in and you can't get it out."
TEACHER:	And it doesn't come out, right? It doesn't work out like a sliver will work back out. But glass doesn't. Glass keeps cutting and going, and this guy's got a whole back full. And listen, this is fantastic. I'm glad you're here right after lunch. They try to take him out of the city, see. He's got this back full of glass. It's still in there. They put him on this cart, belly down, with the glass and then they try to take him along a street that was like out in the front of school.
STUDENT:	"Blacktop."
TEACHER:	"Blacktop. Asphalt. And the asphalt heated up from that bomb drop and it's soupy and the road where it isn't blacktop is, it erupted and so they're gong soup, soup, soup, soup, soup, and they go over a bump and they tip him off and that poor sucker. He lands on his . . . "
STUDENT:	"Back."
TEACHER:	"Back, and it drives the glass even farther in. Poor Cieslik. Oh, I shouldn't get off on that. OK, any other guys?"

In some ways, of course, this episode resembles the discussion in the upper-track classroom in its basic dimensions. Students' turns are short, and the teacher's are long. The student's responses, in fact, can be seen as slotting into a framework that the teacher is building each time she holds the floor. She builds the framework by acknowledging or repeating a student's contribution ("All right, Cieslik"), moving on to a longer stretch of exposition ("I think Cieslik is going to come out bad"), and then closing with a question ("Do you know anything about getting a piece of glass in your skin?").

But it is the nature of that framework that distinguishes the discussion from the one we examined earlier. Here the teacher employs a kind of sophomoric, black humor ("[T]his is fantastic. I'm glad you're . . . " . . . the episode and dramatizing Cieslik's suffering ("soup, soup, soup . . . and they go over a bump and they tip him off and that poor sucker . . . "), John Hersey in a way becomes Stephen King. What is lost, of course, is the serious consideration of human pain that we might expect in a discussion of *Hiroshima*. But the teacher risks that for the opportunity of making vivid to her students the kinds of details that they might otherwise miss. She sacrifices, we might say, a certain measure of literary decorum (precisely the kind of literary decorum we saw in abundance in the upper-track class-room) in exchange for a measure of color and drama. If the teacher working in an upper-track classroom invited his students to regard the text as critics might, here the teacher seems to invite her students to regard the text as they might a television show or a movie. The emphasis is not on form of the text, or even its tone, but on the response of the students to the text—a response that apparently can be elicited only if the text is made familiar, entertaining, and colorful.

The interest in inviting students' responses to the text becomes even clearer when we examine episodes from lower-track classrooms. Here, for example, is a relatively short exchange from a lower-track classroom. The text is the short story "Raymond's Run," and the teacher has just asked her students if they have found any problems in the story.

STUDENT: What do you mean by "problems"?

TEACHER: Oh, problems. See, I guess what I'm thinking of is I found some problems in the story—something that I didn't like that Squeaky said or the way Squeaky thought about something or something that doesn't make sense with you. Is there any problem with the way she tells the story?

> That's what I mean. That's what I'm trying to have you think about.
>
> STUDENT: And write that down on paper?
>
> TEACHER: You got it. How did this story make you feel? What were you feeling when you heard this story?
>
> STUDENT: It didn't make me feel like nothing.

Here again the teacher's role is central. Like teachers working with the upper- and middle-tracks, this teacher speaks more often than her students and takes longer turns. But what a difference in the nature of the talk! From inviting students to take an interest in literary form, we have moved to inviting students to have any interest at all. And in this last episode, that invitation is denied. The role of teachers—supporting, informing, questioning, responding to students' contributions—seems unchanged as we move across the ability levels. The role of students seems similar as well. Their contributions are minimal and almost always made in response to their teachers' agendas. But the substance of the discussion changes so radically across ability levels that it seems almost as if different subjects are being taught under the same name—"Literature." Those different subjects have been insufficiently researched, however, and their long-term effects on students insufficiently understood.

Conclusion

The evidence about the effects of tracking that I have offered in this essay, of course, is anecdotal and only suggestive of the larger patterns that may occur in English classrooms. But the cases I have discussed here are drawn from a much larger series of studies of teachers, students, and classroom discourse (Marshall, 1989; Marshall, Klages, & Fehlman, 1990, 1991). Taken with the findings from other studies of tracking (e.g., Mitchell & Haycock, 1988; Oakes, 1985), the research reported here may begin to provide a more fully developed portrait of how tracking helps shape instruction.

In looking at the attitudes of teachers, for instance, we find that as we move from teachers working with upper-ability classes to teachers working with lower-ability classes that the responsibility for failure falls increasingly on the students themselves. In the upper-ability and middle-ability classrooms that we studied, teachers could point to the pressures on the curriculum or their own professional habits as source of tension and unrealized potential in their instruction. But in the lower-track classroom that we examined here—and it was only one of several that showed similar patterns—the teacher located the source of difficulty in the students. "They are lost," she told us. "They are not readers, and they are tired. And they are angry that they are being asked to read at all."

The students, of course, understand that shift, and as we look in turn at their attitudes, we see an increasing amount of cynicism and anger as we move across the ability levels. Rich, the upper-track student, was able to laugh slyly at the "bottom-of-the-barrel types" and the "dummies." But David—one of those Rich would never have met in class—calls himself a "scumbag" and scorns the indifference and the ignorance of those who imagine for him a conventional range of middle-class opportunities. He seems to understand that somehow he is being blamed for what he doesn't know and can't do, and in his lashing out he indicates that those with power in the school also lack essential knowledge and basic understanding.

Given the profoundly deep nature of these problems and the grave human consequences that seem to follow from them, we might be tempted to view the curricular effects of tracking—the alternative reading lists and the vastly different agendas in classroom discussions—as simply bad teaching. If only teachers were more sensitive, we might say, more willing to take risks, more capable of re-imagining classrooms as communities containing many different voices. But such exercises in teacher bashing are not only naive, they are as insensitive to the lives of teachers as tracking is to the lives of students. Like their students, the teachers we studied are attempting to make their way within an institution that has its own conventions, political pressures, and history. They can no more resist these than their students can; or rather, they can resist them almost precisely as their students do. They can question them; they can laugh about them; they can grow angry about their effects. But in the last analysis the rules—for both teachers and students—are being made someplace else.

It is not teachers who are to blame for tracking, and it is not teachers who can eliminate it or even very successfully minimize its effects. Rather, I think, we must as a larger community re-imagine what schools are for. The system of tracking was developed at the beginning of the twentieth century in response to a specific demographic and economic situation. As we prepare for the twenty-first century, in a vastly different demographic and economic situation, it seems clear that we must begin to design a new system so that a new vision of schooling can begin to be realized.

REFERENCES

Applebee, A.N. (1989). *A study of book-length works taught in high school English courses.* (Report Series 1.2). Albany, NY: Center for the Learning and Teaching of Literature.

Applebee, A.N. (1989). *The teaching of literature in programs with reputations for excellence in English.* (Report Series 1.1). Albany, NY: Center for the Learning and Teaching of Literature.

Goodlad, J. (1984). *A place called school.* New York: McGraw-Hill.

Marshall, J.D. (1989). *Patterns of discourse in classroom discussions of literature.* (Report Series 2.9). Albany, NY: Center for the Learning and Teaching of Literature.

Marshall, J.D., Klages, M.B., & Fehlman, R. (1990). *Discussions of literature in lower-track classrooms.* (Report Series 2.10). Albany, NY: Center for the Learning and Teaching of Literature.

Marshall, J.D., Klages, M.B., & Fehlman, R. (1991). *Discussions of literature in middle-track classrooms.* (Report Series 2.17). Albany, NY: Center for the Learning and Teaching of Literature.

Mitchell, R., & Haycock, K. (1988). Off the tracks. Paper presented at the State Staff Development and Curriculum Conference, Asilomar Conference Center, Pacific Grove, CA.

Oakes, J. (1985). *Keeping track: How schools structure inequality.* New Haven: Yale University Press.

CHAPTER

ON HONESTY IN ASSESSMENT AND CURRICULUM IN LITERATURE

Alan C. Purves
University at Albany, State University of New York

IN THIS PAPER I WILL EXPLORE SOME ISSUES of quality and standards and the assessment of learning in literature. I approach this topic after many years as a classroom teacher of literature and as one who has been involved in large scale assessments including multinational assessments of literature, written composition, and reading (Purves, 1971, 1973, 1984, 1992). In mother tongue education there is a tension between the complexity of what goes on in the classroom or the research enterprise and the demand for a grade or a simple ranking.

When I teach a class in literature, the students and I have read many different selections and have done various things with them: written, read aloud, discussed, sometimes dramatized or filmed. I have lived with the students and watched them change and open themselves to new experience or, sometimes, remain in a rut. Each student has changed from being a name on a roster and a face to a complex reader and a multifaceted individual. We have grown (I would hope) together. Yet at the end of the semester or the course I have had to summarize all of this into a single letter or a number. Similarly, I have worked on developing complex tasks for an assessment based on an analysis of the domain and have developed attitude and background scales in order to analyze the data, only to be asked to come up with a single table that ranks groups of students. "Who is best?" is the question I am asked in both cases.

My plight is paralleled by that of many other teachers. At times we throw up our hands in despair and submit to giving a grade. At times we rail against those tests that give grade or age levels to what our students do and call them insufficient. We deride as ridiculous the claim by teachers that they can tell the difference between a composition with a mark of 77 and one with a mark of 79, but our students ask us to make distinctions that fine. Some among us argue that we cannot even talk about the quality of our students' performance; we can only describe it The same is true of those concerned with large-scale assessment; they resist the idea of a total score in a field like reading or writing and want to make some sort of subscore based on perhaps a division of the content by type of passage read or perhaps a proposed set of skills or abilities. They want to establish descriptive scales rather than a single score that might place one group above or below another.

We know that for many students as well as for others involved in education, the question "How am I doing?" is a valid one that deserves an answer. The student has a vested interest in getting an external judgment to validate her sense of success or failure. The policy-maker and the taxpayer have a vested interest in knowing the value of their investment in education. We cannot deny these legitimate concerns. Should we give them a simple answer or one that respects our sense of the complexity of what we think we do as teachers of literature, whether in our classroom or as a community of teachers at large?

I do not have the answer. Yet, I would like to offer some thoughts based on my experience. They are to be taken as reflections rather than prescriptions.

The first reflection is that I believe most teachers do indeed have standards by which they judge students or themselves. I believe that most large assessments also have sets of standards. Clearly, one set of standards concerns what it is we choose to look at. Our standards are reflected in our test specifications, our questions, and our assignments. We have standards about what is appropriate learning. A student may say, "I have read these books," and we will reply, "Fine, but you should read these." When we make up a test, we select the passages and the questions that we think worthy of being in the test or we decide to ask open-ended rather than multiple-choice questions. We decide to include or exclude questions concerning interests or habits or preferences. All of these decisions we make because we have ideas concerning what is important and what indicates the quality of the program or the student. It is these decisions that I will explore in an effort to help us be more honest with ourselves and our students. I will begin by reiterating some general points concerning my view of the curriculum, then address the special case of literature, and conclude with a few thoughts on portfolio assessment—the current fad.

COMMUNITIES AND MODELS

I believe that a great part of learning in mother tongue is learning the standards and conventions of a particular literate community and thus becoming a part of that community. Nowhere is this more true than in literature, where one learns both a canon and an approved mode of discourse about texts. We learn to approximate models of discourse in certain situations, such as those appropriate in social, academic, or commercial contexts, models of the pragmatics of reading and writing, and models of how to proceed in the activity of reading or writing.

These models persist in all societies and form a part of that which defines a culture. As a person becomes acculturated, that person gathers and assimilates knowledge about text forms, text pragmatics, and procedures for reading and writing texts, much of which is represented within schemata. Included are: knowledge of the lexicon, both oral and in print; knowledge of syntactic structures and of generative rules; knowledge of text structures, such as how stories begin and end or what a paragraph looks like; knowledge of appropriate phrases and other locutions to be used in certain contexts; knowledge of when and under what circumstances it is appropriate to write a particular kind of text or respond to a written text in a particular fashion.

In addition to the knowledge about the world at large, these kinds of knowledge are stored and brought into play in different situations where reading and writing are called for. They serve as models in the individual's head as the individual reads or writes and signal when a particular text that is being written or read meets the demands of the situation. In addition, a literate reader knows when certain texts are to be read and when certain texts are superfluous, as well as when particular written forms are called for or when particular procedures with regard to texts are called for. In short, these models are standards.

Given this complex array of knowledge, a literate individual engages in the activity of reading and writing, thus producing or comprehending and responding to a text. Successful performance depends both upon the knowledge that an individual has and the adeptness in deploying that knowledge. Literacy, then, is not simply a matter of skill or a set of habits but is the use of such skills and habits in a culturally appropriate manner that indicates one has met the standards of a particular literate community, whether the narrow community of members of a discipline or the broader community of a particular society. Literacy is a communal affair involving conventions and standards at many levels, and teachers are usually the conservators of such standards.

By secondary school, students in most countries are aware of many of the norms and standards, such as the importance of handwriting, spelling, and neatness as well as many other norms concerning style, organization, and content and the norms of how to talk in class about a literary text and what questions they will be asked and should ask. Whether they live up to these norms and standards when asked to write a composition or criticize a text is another matter. The important bond they share is a general understanding and acceptance of those norms and standards. Students *know*, by and large, and accept as valued more than they might have the skill to do. They know, for example that one must look for hidden meanings, even if they cannot find any, even if they make the most egregious errors.

The assessment of literature learning (as of all literacy learning), then, is primarily an assessment of the extent to which students have mastered those norms and met those standards. We may say that these norms fall into two broad categories: competence and preference—what students can do and what they "should" choose to do. The distinction is based primarily on the criteria used to assess these two forms of achievement. Competence is usually associated with a set of standards of performance upon which there is some consensus. Preference is usually seen as a set of desired behaviors, upon which there is less consensus as to the criteria and which may be subject to the waves of ideology. Currently fashionable, for example, is that students should choose to review and redraft what they write and do so in a group. Also currently fashionable is that students should choose to share their personal readings of literary texts. The preferences do not usually appear as stated outcomes, although they may appear in some printed curricula (Purves, 1971, 1984); as Heath (1982) observes, preference may indeed be the most important aspect of the reading and writing curriculum.

CULTURE AND ASSESSMENT

Assessment is the determination of the extent to which an individual student or group of students has mastered the conventions, that is, has met the standards. Assessment of learning in the mother tongue focuses on the performance of students in the acts of reading and writing, and most particularly on the products that emerge from those performances—student texts (usually written). Given this focus of assessment, teachers and others conducting assessments need to be concerned with the nature of the tasks they assign and the nature of the criteria they use to judge those tasks.

But we must beware of what we are doing when we assess student learning in school literacy. The construct that we call "reading literature" must be seen in a cultural context and not considered a general cognitive capacity or activity. Even a seeming consensus on goals and aims in literature instruction masks a variation both in ideology of schools and teachers and in instructional practices. However superficially similar, the kinds of tasks assigned, the approaches to instruction, and the ways by which performance is judged are subject to local interpretation.

I have found that when asked about their perceptions of literature learning and writing, students across the United States and other countries have in common a sense of the importance of the product and of the surface features of the product. Yet beneath that commonality exists variation in the perception of what is valued. "Good" compositions from different locales share common qualities of handling of content and appropriateness of style, but such qualities bespeak local characteristics in organization, use of detail, and other aspects of rhetoric. "Good" reading of literature means being able to answer the questions posed by the teachers. Standards of good writing and good answers to questions on literature are interpreted differently in different systems of education, in different schools, and in different assessments. These standards are also applied more or less stringently in judging the actual performance. All of these findings suggest that performance in "reading literature," is a part of a culture and that schools tend to foster interpretive and rhetorical communities.

Performing an assessment of student learning, raises questions about the assumptions concerning the models of literate activity and performance that prevail in a community. It further raises the question that literature learning is not the unitary construct that many national assessments and research studies would have. We should beware talking too superficially about concepts like performance or ability. Performance and ability are task-dependent and culture-dependent as well. We cannot say that someone is a better reader or writer than someone else. All we can say is at this particular time we think person A wrote a good composition on this poem or read this novel according to criteria that we set forth. If we keep this point in mind, we may make more honest assessments.

ASSESSING THE DOMAIN OF LITERATURE

A major function of literature education is the development of what one might call preferences or habits of mind in reading literary texts and particularly in the content of what is written about the texts that have been read. Currently, one must learn what occurred when one has read a text "aesthetically" and to differentiate the discourse about social studies texts from that about poetry. The latter discussion is to include a display of knowledge about literary terms and texts as well as about one's personal readings and critical interpretations of the text. In addition, literature education is supposed to develop something called "taste," or the love of "good literature," so that literature education goes beyond reading and writing to the inculcation of specific sets of preferred habits of reading and writing.

Like any school subject, literature involves public acts in which the student must be more articulate about procedures and strategies as well as conclusions than might be true of the subject outside of school. Proofs are not necessary in mathematical applications outside of school; essays about one's reading of a text are not required after reading every library book or magazine story.

Since literature education is supposed to develop taste, the curriculum looks beyond reading and writing to the formation of specific sets of preferences and habits in those areas. It may include the development of tolerance for a variety of literature, of willingness to acknowledge that many different kinds and styles of work can be thought of as literature, and of acceptance that a reader's not liking a certain text or poem does not mean that the work is not good. The development of such habits of mind should lead students to the acceptance of cultural diversity in literature and, by extension, in society.

The curriculum can also lead students to developing a taste based on an awareness of the meretricious, or shoddy, use of sentiment or language. Experienced readers of literature can see that they are being tricked by a book or a film even when the trickery is going on—and they can enjoy the experience. Like advertising and propaganda, literature manipulates the reader or viewer. The conscious student can be aware of such manipulation and value the craft at the same time as discerning the motives that lie behind it.

To those who would argue that I have been setting forth a view of the curriculum that is not covered in their syllabus or philosophy, I would argue that, however they view their literature program, what they teach and how they teach it will impact—positively or negatively—on the students' knowledge (or ignorance), their performance as readers and writers, and their habits and preferences. If not my specifics, then specifics like them. It is better to be conscious of the interaction of these three effects than to ignore any of them. You cannot have one of the three without the other two.

Putting the pieces of the domain together rationally would suggest that if teachers want to measure their students' learning they will have to attend not only to issues of comprehension and writing about literary texts but also to knowledge, attitudes, and judgments. This means asking the students what they think and feel abut what they have read and also asking them whether they know something about literature as an art. Asking these questions might well alert students to our strong belief in the power of literature to move the mind and to affect our lives. We might also ask them how they value literature and the ideals concerning literature that society professes to hold under the First Amendment as well as under other protestations concerning the value of literature and the arts in our society. When we ask these questions as well as the cognitive ones, we find that we can better see the effects of our teaching. One study has shown that there is little difference in the cognitive outcome of a traditional critical program and a response-centered one; the difference lies in the positive effect the latter has on habits, attitudes, and beliefs (Ho, 1988).

SETTING STANDARDS IN LITERATURE

Let us now turn our attention specifically to standards in the school subject of literature. A prospective description of the dimensions and difficulty levels in literature learning may be seen in Figure 7.1, which is based upon a standard-setting exercise conducted in the summer of 1991 with a group of English language arts teachers (K–12) in British Columbia. This is not a universal set of dimensions and levels but one set in a particular province at a particular time. I cannot prescribe the content—only the process—to those who live and work in other communities at other times. Each must define their own provinciality. The levels of difficulty are based on what we judged as currently known about development and learning. I should emphasize that setting these standards does not set the nature of the assessment or the kinds of tasks that might be exemplars to show that the standards have been met.

The dimensions set forth in Figure 7.1 derive both from one group's definition of the domain of literature learning and from the latent indices of quality and maturity of performance in school literature they perceived. We must, of course, view literature within the broader contexts of reading and writing. In the main, this is because much of what is involved in school literature is related to the broader reading program and, most particularly, demands a variety of written expression, much of it formal. What is special about school literature is the focus on aesthetic reading and response, on the accumulation of texts into a personal canon, and on the viewing of the text as one of the arts. While some of the dimension headings therefore resemble those in reading, there is clearly a special edge to them that focuses on the aesthetic and the literary.

The first dimension deals with the application of various kinds of knowledge, from the more immediate and personal to the more abstract. Of course, acquiring the knowledge is important, but we do not value it in and of itself, only as it is brought into play in the practice of reading and articulating the response to what is read. Some cultures, of course, value knowledge for itself, the knowledge, in particular, that appears to define the culture for what it is. Again, however, many would argue that this knowledge must be put into

> **FIGURE 7.1**

Dimensions and Standards in Literature Learning

DIMENSION
Basic
2
3
4
Advanced

A good student applies knowledge
Personal experience
Genres
Terminology
Background and cultural
Theoretical

A good student selects literary material according to established principles
Written over oral
Varied subjects
Complex
Mature
Classic

A good student articulates a reasoned understanding of the literary text
Clear
Elaborated and detailed
Consistent
Acknowledging alternatives
Abstract

A good student reflects upon the reading from personal and critical perspectives
Personal experience as analogy
Person implication; generic relationships
Distinction between personal and public implications
Personal relationship as a metaphor; critical issues that may arise
Place of the text in the broader context of literature and culture

A good student moves easily among the varied types of literary text
Personal/school
Literary/nonliterary
Varied genres
Extensive and intensive readings
Contextualized and decontextualized texts

A good student participates in a community of readers
Shares responses
Accepts responses of others
Modifies responses in the light of those of others
Summarizes responses of a group
Takes group responses and reformulates

A good student shares in public values concerning the role of literature and the arts in society
Distinguishes personal and public criteria for judging texts
Recognizes levels/types of taste
Recognizes cultural contributions
Recognizes issues concerning arts policy
Supports literature and the arts

use in order to assess the understanding of the individual. One could then assess the knowledge separately, but I would argue that it is best to assess its application. The knowledge dimension includes textual, cultural, and critical knowledge.

The second dimension concerns the selection of material, which appears to be important within many programs. One of the major aims of literature instruction is to develop the habit of reading aesthetically and the habit of reading certain texts rather than others. We want students not only to read but to read a variety of texts and eventually to read that which is most clearly sanctioned by the establishment. This dimension is tempered by democratic tendencies on the part of many teachers and curriculum makers who advocate breadth without selection, but the idea of selection clearly enters the secondary school curriculum and the assessments contained therein.

The third dimension concerns the articulation of a response to a literary text. Reading literature is not to be done in isolation from other activities, including individual and group discussion, writing, and other forms of displaying understanding. It is also clear that as a student progresses through the curriculum the articulation of the response should be the product more of reason than of passion, although there is a desired vestige of the emotional and personal. Classroom talk, and particularly writing, should become more "civilized," should come under the sway of logic and seeming objectivity. It should move into the realm of public academic discourse. I no longer make the case that this discourse must follow a particular critical or theoretical school for the simple reason that (at least in North America), none of these schools are in the ascendant.

The fourth dimension refers to the reflectiveness of the reader in discourse about the text. As in other reading, the reflection can be personal or critical, and the levels refer to the increasing abstractness of the reflection, the widening circle of the transaction between reader and text. The text does not become depersonalized for the reader but exists in an ever widening sphere of personal and literary knowledge. This is evidenced primarily in talk or writing, but it may also be evidenced in the choices of the next book to read or in other forms of expression or participation in literature.

The fifth dimension relates literature to the broader field of reading and textual studies. It is clear that different texts serve different functions and that students are expected to develop expertise in moving from fiction to poetry to nonfiction to textbooks and adjust their way of reading and reporting about the reading as they make these moves. Initially, students are expected to differentiate texts read for personal pleasure from those to be read for the purpose of articulating a response in school. They are not to devalue either, for both are encouraged, particularly in elementary school where the intention is to set reading habits. Nonetheless, the approach to the text that is to be discussed in groups or conferences differs from that to the text that is to be read for oneself. As the student moves through school, this difference extends to one between those that are to be read "for background" and those that are to be read more intensively. At an even more advanced level is the distinction between those texts that are to be read in their full context of biographical, historical, and critical information and those that are to be read in a less highly contextualized manner. The first are the kinds of text that a student is to "master" or to read in depth. This is a kind of reading that occurs seldom until upper secondary school.

The final dimension refers to the shared values concerning the role of literature and the arts in society. We expect the student to begin to recognize the difference between personal and public values. "It's good, but I don't like it" may be the first indication that there are values outside of personal preference and that the student recognizes their existence. This then can lead to the acknowledgment of levels of taste and quality. The idea of good books may lead to the idea of those books being a part of what shapes a culture (not that the others don't shape another part of the culture). From here to a respect for the rights of the book and the artist and to active support of the arts through contributions and other acts represents another level of commitment to shared public values.

The dimensions and standards that we have set forth are broadly applicable to students at various stages in school; the fifth standard might not be reached by many students below the university level, but it has been my experience that it may be reached by the student who undertakes a research project, who becomes heavily involved in the school literary magazine or theater, who becomes an "expert" on a particular writer or genre. These standards, are such that we might see level 1 as comprising a basic level, levels 2 and 3 as a proficient one, and levels 4 and 5 as an advanced one. Further division of the levels is probably not necessary.

Within such a framework, we may then use varied means of assessment, including logs, interviews, performances, and other pieces of what might go into an assessment package or a portfolio for a student or group of students. Without specifying the assessment, they provide a set of ground rules for judging performance within a dimension and the level of difficulty that has been attained. We need, or course, to look at a task and our judgment of performance on that task to set it within one or more dimensions.

CREATING COMPREHENSIVE MEASURES AND PORTFOLIO ASSESSMENT

A comprehensive measure of student performance will address each of the standards and allow for varied levels of performance. Within knowledge, for example, textual knowledge and knowledge of critical terms are distinct, particularly in their relationship to the practice of reading and responding. Although in pedagogy such knowledge is integrated into practice, for assessment purposes it may be important to see if students have the knowledge as well as whether they use it. Within the domain of practice, more than one passage is needed to get some estimate of a student's performance across text types. It makes little difference whether one uses open-ended or multiple-choice questions, but one can argue on other grounds that open-ended questions present more of a challenge to students than multiple-choice questions (Hansson, 1991), and are a more exacting measure of the ability to read and shape a response to what is read.

It is also clear that extended responses are also desirable, but other studies argue that the phrasing of the question might be such as to allow the student some preparation for the setting forth of a fully articulated composition. A stark question is less desirable than a question that builds upon another sort of "mediating task," one that gets the student to consider the text in question and acts as a starter for the discourse (Hansson, 1991). Some combination of choice or scale, essay, and performance may form the optimum measure. In the realm of preference, it is important to separate the student's criteria for judging a text from the actual judgment. It is also important to get a depiction of the general attitudes towards literature including censorship, since these are related to cognitive performance (whether in an antecedent or consequent role remains unclear).

A broad view of assessment gives a more comprehensive picture of a student learning and also of program effectiveness than does a measure of any one taken alone. If the intention of the instruction is to make classroom exploration of literature more open and to use more "real" and thought-provoking questioning than normal instruction, its validation must include measures of both practice and preference. The development and trial of an assessment package to serve as a model at the state or district level, and at the classroom level, is the next step and should be combined with setting standards.

Recently, there has been a call to move away from the single test or grade to what has come to be called the portfolio approach to assessment. In this type of assessment, there is gathered for each student a collection of materials, both trial attempts and finished products. The range of materials has theoretically been broad, but in practice it has comprised mostly written records, either compositions by the student or some sort of log of activities recorded by student or teacher. The portfolio has been heralded as a good way of monitoring "student progress." It has also been used to show the nature and quality of a school's program. In some cases, districts and even states have used portfolios. Even some of the advocates of portfolios have questioned whether they can be used for any sort of summary judgment of performance, that purpose that rules most tests and assessment programs.

Let me say that I believe that they can be so used and that in fact they are so used. Portfolios are no more and no less than a collection of student performances. In most cases these performances have been judged either by the students themselves or by some external jury. They provide a reflection of both what the school has asked the student to do and of the student's "success" in fulfilling that expectation. Such a definition holds true whether the portfolio contain exemplars of only the "best" and "finished" work or of work in progress. Portfolios should reflect the principles I have set forth in earlier sections of this paper. In particular, the portfolio gives us a good portrait of the standards, conventions, and models of performance in literature that the teacher, school, or district espouses. To my mind the portfolio should serve as a check on whether we are limiting our perspective of performance too greatly. There has been a tendency to focus the entire school language arts program on reading contemporary trade literature or on writing personal narratives and expressive pieces of writing. The practice of keeping portfolios raises the possibility that as teachers we do not drift too far in this direction just as we should not drift too far in relying wholly on standardized multiple-choice tests.

Our assessment of student learning in literature, then, should be broad, should focus on performance in many areas, should be carefully constructed, and should be set forth and reported with a clear sense of the arbitrary nature of our tasks, our standards and the ways in which they reflect our particular small piece of the world of literature. We should make no great claims either in our assessment or in our curriculum.

REFERENCES

Hansson, G. (1991). Reading and understanding literature. In A. C. Purves, (Ed.), *The idea of difficulty in literature*. Albany, NY: SUNY Press.

Heath, S. B. (1983). *Ways with words*. New York: Cambridge.

Ho, B. (1988). *An investigation of two methods of teaching poetry to secondary students*. Unpublished masters thesis, National University of Singapore, Singapore.

Purves, A.C. (1971). Evaluation of learning in literature. In B.S. Bloom, J.T. Hastings, & G. Madaus (Eds.), *Handbook of formative and summative evaluation of student learning*. New York: McGraw-Hill.

Purves, A.C. (1973). *Literature education in ten countries: An emperical study. International studies in evaluation*. Stockholm: Almqvist and Wiksell.

Purves, A.C. (1984). The potential and real achievement of U.S. students in school reading. *American Journal of Education, 93*, 82–106.

Purves, A.C. (Ed.). (1992 in press). *The IEA study of written composition II: Instruction and achievement*. Oxford: Pergamon Press.

CHAPTER 8

LITERATURE AND PUBLIC POLICY

James R. Squire
Retired, Marlborough, New Hampshire

ADDRESSING THE OPENING SESSION OF THE 1990 NCTE convention, author Shay Youngblood reminded us that art and politics don't mix, a sentiment expressed repeatedly throughout history from the time that Plato first banished the poets from his imaginary republic because of his fear of literature's capacity to raise the emotions, to tap the irrational in each of us, to educate our uncontrollable imaginations. Such attitudes continue to this day. Witness Senator Jesse Helm's recent campaign against the National Endowment for the Arts.

Controversy seems to be an inevitable consequence of establishing public policy with respect to the teaching and learning of literature; and yet we have seen continued attempts to link the two:

1. In the effort to fill early nineteenth century readers with moralistic if not religious snippets in a conscious attempt to ensure that the Priscillas and Johns of that day became better human beings;

2. In the well-documented efforts of Nazi Germany during the thirties to force school children to read literature that seemed to support their myths of a superrace;

3. In the emphasis in our country and in most others of a strong sampling of indigenous patriotic literature (sometimes of dubious literary distinction) to convey the values of the culture. Who can think the thoughts of Lincoln unless nourished on the same food?

Used in these ways, literature contributes to the shaping of public attitudes. Some of us will recall during the recent past the often bitter struggle of Canadian teachers and Canadian writers to present Canadian literature, not foreign literature, in their school programs.

Because literature presents ideas and ideals more readily and more effectively than any other subject taught in school—this because it taps the heart as well as the head—society must see that selections are read and taught that reflect the essence of a society.

But the values of a state or nation can change, and with such change come demands that the program in literature change— today, Anglo, Asian American, Latino, and African American literary traditions; tomorrow, perhaps Islamic. Time and conditions continually change, and so does public policy.

Thirty years ago, when we pressed so vigorously for extending the National Defense Education Act to include English, the greatest stumbling block in seeking approval in the United States Congress was the literary content of our subject. "What? All that money for the teaching of poetry?" commented one incredulous senator to NCTE president Harold B. Allen.

English teachers preparing proposals for federal scrutiny were then cautioned against mentioning a single literary work by name—not in curriculum development projects, not in proposals for teacher institutes. The content of proposals in those days was seen as grist for congressional debate over federal support of the arts, and the vision of a powerful senator like Barry Goldwater waving "objectionable" books like *Catcher in the Rye* or John Dos Passos's *U.S.A. Trilogy* on the floor of the Senate caused bureaucrats in the Office of Education to quiver.

What a difference twenty-five years makes! A Republican administration only a few years ago not only established a National Center for the Learning and Teaching of Literature but encouraged an Assistant Secretary of Education to define exactly what children should read. Witness the work of Chester Finn and Diane Ravitch in *What Do Our Seventeen Year-Olds Know?* and particularly their manipulation of data in a national assessment as part of their personal report. And it seems no accident that Lynne Cheney's *American Memory*, E.D. Hirsch's *Cultural Literacy*, and even the California literature-based school program emerged from the same cauldron of simmering ideas. Yet the fact remains that widespread and indiscriminate use of many trade books in the classroom—part and parcel of the call—soon ran into community resistance when parents in many areas found some elements in certain books that conflicted with their ethical, moral, or religious beliefs. It is no accident that 85 percent of all citizen objections to required reading of a particular book in school are to library, or trade books. Literary anthologies and classroom readers are generally compiled to avoid the more sensitive concerns, and the all-out commitment to children's literature in California (commendable in many ways) seem initially uninformed by what we know about the importance of instructional experience with all significant modes of writing, particularly biography and expository prose. Reading and writing only narrative and expressive prose is not sufficient to develop a full literacy.

But widespread concern nationally with children's literature as a priority of elementary level education has only just begun. We can be thankful to Bill Honig (past Superintendent of Public Instruction, California State Department of Education) for his concern with literature in the primary school classroom; otherwise children's books might be receiving as little attention in the total curriculum as they had earlier. Indeed, not until 1987 was there a National Literature Center at all, and only since the present renewal grant has the Center for the Learning and Teaching of Literature been empowered to deal with literature below the secondary school level. Fortunately, this overly narrow concern with literature as solely a secondary school academic subject has now been rectified.

But the omission illuminates the essential problem inherent in literature and public policy. Unlike the development of competence in reading and writing, which are instantly seen by the public as defining basic literacy (and hence essential to all learning and to bedrock subjects that must be emphasized if schooling is to prepare our young people to become scientists, mathematicians, and technologists capable of competing with the Germans and Japanese), literature seems unrelated to the central goals of literacy. Indeed, so unrelated to the central goals of literacy, as defined by most public figures, does literature appear to curriculum specialists that literary study and literary scholarship, save for the obligatory nod to multicultural content, did not even appear in the proposed strategic guidelines for the National Council of Teachers of English distributed to directors during the 1990 meeting. Strategies adopted by an organization like NCTE are another statement of public policy.

Literature and public policy? What public policies can possibly govern the literature selection for reading in religious schools, whether Catholic, Lutheran, or any other denomination? And yet teachers in religious schools are clearly right to demand a literary content that presents their religious values.

Literature and public policy? How, when legal advisors consistently inform us that we have no legal right to require any child to read any particular title if the title is objectionable to the parent of the child on any reasonable basis? Better to select an alternative for that particular child, yet not for his classmate who may have parents with very different values.

A public policy on literature? How, when, according to Ed Jenkinson, we have 240 organized pressure groups trying to influence what should be included and excluded from the curriculum?

A public policy on literature when, according to the Center for the Learning and Teaching of Literature, our nation's high school teachers are still teaching the same literature selections that occupied their attention thirty years ago—despite the herculean efforts of African Americans, feminists, and Latinos to expand the traditional Anglo-American literary curriculum?

A public policy for literature when most high school teachers understand little of what has transpired among literary theorists and literary critics over the past three decades, including the vitally important work in reader response? The teachers of many still seem embedded in the textual analyses of the New Criticism three decades after this approach has largely been abandoned by most literary scholars and those engaged in literary inquiry.

No. Better to have public policy, whether at state or national levels, dealing with *literacy*, not *literature*. They are not the same. Affirm its importance, of course, but let decisions in what and how to teach remain with the classroom teacher in the local community setting.

Afferent (aesthetic) experience *in*, *through*, and *with* literature cannot be legislated, and any attempt to impact the teaching of literature from an external limited base will create more problems than we need.

REFERENCES

Anderson, R., Hiebert, E.H., Scott, J.A., and Wilkinson, I.A.G. (1985). *Becoming a nation of readers: The report of the Commission on Reading.* Washington, DC: National Institute of Education.

Applebee, A. (1989). *The teaching of literature in programs with reputations for excellence in English.* Albany, NY: Center for the Learning and Teaching of Literature.

Barr, M. (1991). The California Literature Curriculum. E.J. Farrell & J.R. Squire (Eds.), *In Transactions with literature: A fifty-year perspective.* Urbana, IL: National Council of Teachers of English.

Cheney, L.V. (1987). *American memory.* Washington, DC: National Endowment for the Humanities.

Hirsch, E.D. (1987). *Cultural literacy: What every American needs to know.* Boston: Houghton Mifflin.

Jenkinson, E.B. (1979). *Censors in the classroom: The mind benders.* Carbondale, IL: Southern Illinois University Press.

Nelms, B. (Ed.) (March 1977). Multicultural literature. *English Journal,* 75.

Ravitch, D., & Finn, C. (1987). *What do our seventeen year-olds know?* New York: Harper & Row.

Smith, N.B. (1934, 1986). *American reading instruction.* Newark, DE: International Reading Association.

Venezky, R., et al. (1987). *The subtle danger.* Princeton, NJ: Educational Testing Service.

CHAPTER 9

WINDS OF CHANGE IN LITERATURE EDUCATION

James Flood and Diane Lapp

San Diego State University

THE DECADE OF THE 1980s BROUGHT substantive changes to the teaching of literature in American elementary and secondary classrooms. Innovations in literary theory, instructional practices, text selection, assessment, and national and local policy regarding the teaching of literature caused changes to occur at every level of education. Although changes did occur, they were neither monolithic nor universal. Widespread change is often a slow process that occurs as the result of widespread dissemination of the beneficial effects of the innovation. This dissemination has yet to occur in the area of literature education.

In the case of literature instruction, five areas of change have dominated research findings during the past ten years: (1) literary theory in which the emphasis shifted from the "correct" interpretation of text to reader-based meaning construction; (2) instructional practices in which students created meaning through multiple readings as well as social exchanges with peers and adults; (3) text selection in which teachers, students, and publishers broadened their definition of quality literature to include texts written by and about a wide variety of people, events, and phenomena; (4) assessment in which the readers' processes of building meaning were acknowledged and valued, and (5) national and local policy that emphasized the value of "quality" literature for every child. (see California English/Language Arts Framework, 1987)

But what of future change? We believe that our notions of appropriateness and value in literature education will continue to grow with new knowledge of how students learn best. But, for the present, we are in need of a theory of instruction that balances our understanding of process learning, in which students are encouraged to construct on-going meaning, with our understanding of teaching roles, such as mentoring, modeling, and conferring.

But why hasn't such a theory of literature instruction been developed? And why hasn't appropriate instruction followed? Farrell (1991) noted that although three curriculum models serve as the rationale for most literature instruction (a mastery model, a heritage model, and a process model) only one model, the process model, will serve response-based literature instruction. But, he notes, this model has not yet surfaced as the dominant form of instruction for literature in today's classrooms.

Applebee (1991) and Langer (this volume) explain this phenomenon by pointing to educator's inability (or timidity) to embrace a process model. They maintain that our progress in writing/composition instruction, which is constantly working toward increased understanding of how implementation can effectively take place, is in direct contrast to our progress in literature instruction. They contend that educators are wary to give up what they know best and tend to revert to mastery and heritage models of instruction that stress correct interpretations of texts. They maintain that, even while process activities such as discussion and book talks are dominating a great deal of the inquiry about literature instruction, the quest for the "right interpretation" of texts still dominates teaching and learning activities in many classrooms, whether they are first-grade classrooms in which children are encouraged to "learn" the stories' lessons or secondary classrooms in which students are invited to "understand" great authors' works by reading what the critics have said about the meaning of their texts.

In this volume, Blau speaks about teachers' willingness to use process approaches with writing instruction and their unwillingness to use them with literature. He explains how secondary literature teachers in his project were reluctant to be cooperative, supportive, and flexible as they attempted to socially construct meaning while interpreting literary texts. This reluctance was in sharp contrast to the ease and comfort that characterized their participation in writing groups.

While this discrepancy is perplexing, it is not inexplicable. We hypothesize that teachers are ready to explore and use process instruction in writing because they have been convinced of its benefits from years of personal experimentation *and* by the results of a wide variety of research studies that convinced them that children become more fluent and more engaged writers when they are permitted frequent opportunities to write and discuss their writing—when they have opportunities to share, to expand, and to witness the importance of writing. We also contend that process instructional approaches to writing have been so successful because teachers see a clear role for themselves—a richly diverse role that includes mentoring, advising, and modeling.

Process writing instruction has also been successful because assessment of writing has changed dramatically and has (astoundingly) kept pace with innovative notions of writing instruction. Assessment has not held writing instruction hostage; it has not held writing instruction captive to previous notions of appropriateness and value. In fact, changes in writing instructional approaches caused educators to demand changes in assessment that require real/authentic writing as the only reliable means of assessment.

These three variables—(1) time (for evidence to amass and for familiarity and practice with new instructional ideas); (2) clearly defined roles for teachers and students; (3) assessment initiatives (that parallel instructional advances)—seem to be some of the most critical factors that are needed for change to take place.

In the field of literature instruction many of the critical pieces for long-term change are in place, especially in the areas of materials and management. For example, we have become increasingly aware of a variety of books that are available for students at all levels, and we have become knowledgeable about the effects of grouping patterns, response modes, and time needed for group discussions, for in-class and out-of-class reading and for read-alouds.

But what has not yet occurred in literature instruction is (1) allowing ample time to elapse for success stories to emerge; (2) the generation of clearly defined roles for students and teachers during literature instruction; and (3) the development of appropriate assessment techniques.

TIME FOR SUCCESS STORIES

As evidence of the effectiveness of process approaches in literature instruction begins to mount, change will begin to take place in many different schools. The success stories offered in this volume by Langer, Roser, Blau, and Purcell-Gates are only some of the successes that have been reported in recent years about the benefits of permitting students ample opportunities for constructing interpretations of texts that evolve and grow from multiple readings as well as discussions with peers and adults.

However, until teachers are presented with mounds of convincing data that time spent in classrooms on discussion and rereading is time well spent, they are right to wonder about response-based process approaches to instruction. Fortunately, the evidence is mounting, and it is coming in the form of anecdotes, case studies, and testimonials by students and teachers as well as in quantitative studies that measure recall, interpretation, and appreciation.

CLEARLY DEFINED ROLES FOR STUDENTS AND TEACHERS

In previous models of literature instruction, student and teacher roles were extremely clear. Teachers presented interpretations and asked questions about these interpretations, which students answered. (With young children and students acquiring reading skills, teachers also taught decoding and comprehension strategies.)

In reader-response-based classrooms, the roles for students and teachers have expanded enormously. Students become meaning makers (not interpretation receivers); they construct meaning socially through reading, rereading, reflecting, and sharing with adults and peers in their classrooms. They begin to realize that interpretation is idiosyncratic and evolving; it is an "envisionment" that continues to grow (Langer, this volume).

Teacher's roles have also expanded. In addition to new roles for classroom management, as explained by Roser (this volume) and Marshall (this volume), teachers also have new roles as text selectors whose growing knowledge makes them increasingly aware of the rich variety of books that are available. As our understanding of instructional scaffolding as a metaphor for good teaching grows (Applebee, 1991), teacher's roles change to providing help when needed, providing appropriately stimulating questions that advance understanding of texts, and providing alternative interpretations.

ASSESSMENT

As Purves (this volume) suggests, previous assessments of literature knowledge were restricted to evaluations of student's knowledge of plot and characterization. While such knowledge is critical, it is only a small piece of what needs to be assessed in literature. New forms of assessment, including performance and portfolio assessment, need to be developed that will enable students and teachers to understand the ways in which students develop insights and interpretations. This type of assessment is beginning to be developed in the field of writing; efforts to develop similar assessment techniques in literature need to be encouraged.

WINDS OF CHANGE: A FINAL NOTE

Substantial change has already occurred in literature instruction, and it continues to occur daily in classrooms. But the truly significant change that is necessary for all students to become engaged with literature has not yet occurred in any widespread manner. In order for this to occur, three things need to happen:

1. ample time has to elapse for success stories to amass;

2. roles for students and teachers have to be clearly defined;

3. assessment initiatives that are compatible with response-based literature teaching have to be developed.

As in the case of writing instruction, when these three variables are in place, literature instruction will change dramatically for the better with real emphasis on students creating understandings of texts through social interactions with peers and adults.

REFERENCES

Applebee, A. (1991). *Environments for language teaching and learning.* In J. Flood, J. Jensen, D. Lapp, and J. Squire (Eds.), *Handbook of research in teaching the English language arts.* New York: Macmillan.

English/language arts framework. (1987). Sacramento: California Department of Education.

Farrell E. (1991). Instructional models for English language arts, k–12. In J. Flood, J. Jensen, D. Lapp, and J. Squire (Eds.), *Handbook of research in teaching the English language arts.* New York: Macmillan.

INDEX